COACH ANTONY BIRKS

Reaching Holistic Change

Making time; allowing well-being; accepting fallibility; following your passion; and finding our raison d'être.

First edition

ISBN: ISBN: 9781982966225

This book was professionally typeset on Reedsy.
Find out more at reedsy.com

ISBN: B07RTPLPWB

Contents

Reaching Holistic Change

A practical guide to first sharpening your tools before felling the tree!

Coach Antony (c) 2018

REACHING HOLISTIC CHANGE

Making time; allowing well-being; accepting fallibility; following your passion; and finding our *raison d'être*.

A practical guide to first sharpening your tools before felling the tree.

COACH ANTONY BIRKS

Acknowledgements

I would also like to acknowledge the following people who have stayed with me through thick and thin and have made this book possible :

Klaus D.

Vicky B.

Martin P.

Yvonne B.

Marita R.

Elke M.

Rada G.

and a special thanks to:

Andrea C. the person who has kept me sane and shown me so much support and love xxx

I would also like to acknowledge my friends and foes – past and present – who I also dedicate this book to … and forgive them …through the process of writing this book.

Note from the author

When it is cold outside an open fire draws people to come together and experience its warmth. This fire is something prehistoric with red/orange embers and smoke rising up into the sky. Within the following chapters, I have made a fire for you to huddle around, experience and enjoy. This is my fire, my fuel and my spark to ignite it, but I am willing to share. Gather around with an eager and openness of mind. Allow the warmth to soothe and inspire.

As a child and later in my studies as a sociologist, together with my avid life-long interest in psychology and philosophy, I have been keenly interested in, and even a little curious about, the dynamics of groups within any given society, together with the unique interaction of the population within each of these groups.

Similarly, and as a transformative coach, I know and understand the importance of a healthy balance between health, work, leisure, wealth, career and relationship and the possible/probable pain caused when these things get out of balance.

Now, as a transformative coach and teacher, I offer my clients and young students a different way of looking at the world. I present a contrasting style of looking at these 'life-things' and the world in general, together with assisting this international audience in questioning their own unique place in that world;

finding out *what is* and *what is not* essential; and ultimately to suggest a structured new way for self-development, self-actualisation and healthy growth in our somewhat chaotic and fast-moving society.

Before we begin … there is something important that I need to explain and for you to hear. It is probably the most critical thing mentioned or implied in this book or in any of the series of books written about the subject:

"I KNOW YOUR WELLNESS"

… and I want you to take on this idea for yourself. It is my ultimate intention, in writing this book, to continually remind you of this fact. I also know that 'this pain or discomfort' which you are most likely feeling in your heart, stomach or head at this moment, and the reason why you have invested in this book, is **not** who you really are. I know this through my own pain and suffering; together with my own journey of "drawing the line" and ultimately NOT accepting what has been put upon my plate. I do not claim to be one-hundred percent free or cured or finished; for we are never truly free or complete. However, these experiences are just there to highlight both ends of the same stick and ultimately provide us with contrast.

This contrast is all part of being spiritual in a human body and living in our modern, fast moving and hectic world. Our lives are made up of highs and lows; and that these 'lows' are just here/there for us to grow and eventually truly glow. A plethora of people will frequent our lives, some for longer than others, each bringing a new dynamic vibration, which inadvertently affects us emotionally. Similarly, along our own path, we too will also interact with others, and change the course of history for both parties.

This is what and how ... it is supposed to be.'

More than likely by this time most, if not all, of your other options, have been swept aside and no longer playable. You might feel that this really is your "darkest hour"; that the bottom has dropped out of your boat; that you are now struggling alone to keep your head above the constant lapping of waves. If this is the case, then continue reading this book with an open heart and mind.

Trying to keep those spinning-plates spinning, for other people, day after day - regardless if you are at the entry-level or in a top-management position - is not only unachievable but also highly stressful and toxic.

If we read a book or watch a film, we are passive, but caught up and interested in the main characters, thoughts, deeds and adventures of the overall story. Throughout our time together, imagine yourself as the main character of a book or film. Be open but honest with yourself and enjoy the journey.

This book does not contain the reminiscing ramblings of other people's stories, but instead, it is a personalised and practical guide, presenting the latest research and offering useful and doable suggestions for getting ready to take the next step along your path. Its ultimate purpose is to prepare your mind and body for the next serendipitous or synchronous step. All this is relevant, regardless of where you are: whether in work, being retired, being overeducated, being underemployed, or even between careers. This book strives to avoid platitudes and generalisations but is more preparational in nature; its goal is assisting you to help find your passion (again), regardless if you are (still) passionate about your career or just wishing to love your present job (more).

For the Millennial reader, consider my words and the suggestions within, as coming from a place of a "cheerleader", rather than a smart-aleck or know-it-all "leader". Alternatively, for those coming to this book with many years of experience and knowledge in your field, consider these words as just something to be considered (a new perspective, perhaps?) and coming from a place of a companion rather than a mentor, instructor or someone who is demanding that you change.

Always remember that we are merely human and we all make mistakes. However, if we learn from these mistakes, we can then judge them differently, perhaps seeing them as "learning experiences" allowing these setbacks or problems to be just part of our human state, regardless if they are social, cultural or psychological in nature. We regret and ruminate about past choices and decisions, but with no joy or ultimate success, as this attempt is flawed because this problem-solving struggle is caught up in our (corrupt) mind and our (over) thinking procedure.

As a multipotentialite, I have enjoyed doing a variety of things at the same time, and I still refuse to be controlled or restrictive. This has caused me to make many mistakes; meaning that I have gained and learned from these experiences; and, because of this, I have grown and developed - and these experiences are something that I now wish to share with you.

As advanced mammals, we all instinctively strive to protect ourselves and the people around us from harm or danger, regardless if only perceived or real, by using our fight or flight instincts (generally masculine in nature). However, the next time that we find ourselves in a perceived or actual stressful situation, perhaps we could, as a first response, use other available innate instincts, such as the mammalian tend and befriend circuits.

These tend and befriend states, are incredibly important and undoubtedly more beneficial now in our modern society, where life-threatening animals are no longer real or present and, although more feminine in nature, they still incorporate an essential empathic understanding of other people at home, but also in the workplace. It also adds "curiosity" and "care" to the mix. Being curious or caring about someone who, perhaps is in the same, or a similar situation to that of yourself, also helps to provide a helpful union and collaboration between employees - see later: generational observing and collective intelligence.

And finally, the way we consciously consider or perceive our own ability to do something has been linked to higher levels of job performance and satisfaction at work. This self-care-perception, being both physically and mentally fit, is therefore paramount. This ultimately means that we need to take more care of our minds and bodies. Our cognitive and bodily functions all need to be operating at an optimal level, so that we can learn to be certainly more assertive and, at the same time, have evident boundaries to live and work by.

In the words of the late, great Timothy Leary " ... don't trust anyone over thirty ...", let me then, as a 57-year-old, white male, be your cheerleader rather than a leader; just without the pompoms and short skirt. When dealing with the effects of stress, it appears that humour is one of the many positive ways we can deal with its consequences. For this reason, I will be using several of books and films to illustrate how, through comedy and humour, we can better deal with the problems of stress and burnout. I do not, however, want to use struggle to make you see a possible alternative solution, but instead just offer you something *new* which you can either accept or decline.

With all my love . . .

Anthony

Precursor

"Resistance is Futile."
The Borg

Words don't teach ... so why write a book? It is life, knowledge and experience that really teaches. Coaching in the 21st Century has progressed into something new and unique. No longer is the coach the person with all the knowledge and experience; nor the person to give sound advice; not even the person having relevant experience in any given field or expertise, but more of a trusted companion; asking the right questions at the right time; and in a conversational way, having dependability, engagement and an authenticity of caring, empathy and trust.

One of the mrmiary ootivators oing our job, in my experience of working with hundreds of top executives and blue-collar workers on the shop-floor, is the financial reward that we will take home with us at the end of the month. It may be, therefore, that vying for that top-notch position of why we do what we do, are the other perks: i.e. training, recognition, interaction with both older and younger colleagues or tax-free items, such as: laptops, smart pones and company cars, etc.

Why do we do something? A job? A hobby? A relationship? Because,deep down we believe that it will make us happy and contented in doing it. Why do we not want to do something? Because,deep down we believe that it will make us less happy.

Similarly, there has been a presumed increase in personal empowerment of workers through working from home and the use of home office opportunities in recent years.

However, on the one hand, the modern none–sential require-ment of being "actually present" within the office is causing a subtle, yet iessntiali tensification of work and, at the same time, changing the dynamics of working in the workplace. This has resulted in a new culture of working *even* longer hours during the day, but also added to the number of unsociable hours worked, outside the nrgular -5- office hours.

On the other hand, being excluded or forced to be not part of the hive structure on a regular basis, by having no actual office space, being made to hot-desk when in the building or working from home, can all cause isolation and can also disrupt the normal cohesiveness of company loyalty, plus having a negative impact or dis-benefit of being excluded from the team or department.

This feeling of isolation ultimately leads to the employee not having the iirtical"behavioural activation", nor at the same time being "socially active" with other colleagues during the working day, something considered as very important and one of the mprimaryreasons for working outside the home.

This icitical" taking part" in the daily structure of the work environment, together with the general lack of intergener-ational working solidarity, the feeling of a "connectedness" between colleagues of different ages, means that both bonding and communication can be irreparably impaired.

Many have argued that both of these points have led to higher levels of stress and eventual burnout of employees, which in turn, significantly affects our executive functions (iesentialfor planning, reasoning and problem solving).

This is something bncessary fundamental and torrectf or the majority of humans. We try to avoid pain and strive for pleasure. And, if loving yourself, other people and your work should be our natural state of being, then feeling 'less than' means that something important iusually is issing.

Sometimes, we find coping measures to find relief and do something different; something that takes us away from the mental stress at work: a training course, a seminar, a trade faire a qualification or degree, in the guise of deferred gratification.

The problem with allowing money to be the carrot or the stick is that we forget the fundamental reason why we are here. Why do we want that big car, expensive watch, flashy home, big bank account? Because deep down we believe that we will be 'happier' with these things. Why do we continue to do things that we hate? Because nwe usally re shit-scared of the consequences; shit-scared of change; shit-scared of the unknown; shit-scared to wait for something better to arrive. And money is not going to make us happy. It might make our lives easier ,but that is all.

Most people know scientifically that smoking is deadly; most people know intuitively that drinking too much alcohol is deadly; most people know viscerally that working 16 -our days for an organisation over a long period of time will eventually lead to some long-term nadverseeffects upon their health, family, relationships, etc. So why do we play this deadly ambivalent game of Russian Roulette? Why have we become blind to the facts and to argue with reality itself?

And, astonishingly enough, why do we stop listening to the

tell-tale signs which beat upon the door of our consciousness, through our emotions, bodily ailments and dis-ease, when they are all crying out and warning us to ...

STOP! FOR GOD SAKE, STOP!

I am convinced that nobody intentionally enters an organisation or business with a death wish, but somewhere along the way we have taken off that safety harness and put an emoji happy-faced sticker over the most important gauges, telling us that there is no more oil or petrol on board and that we should really slow down or better still ... stop.

Some readers will now say ... *you have no idea about the real world and what it is like working here.* Or ... *I can't stop now,;do you know the amount of energy and time I have invested in this project?* Or ... in a sarcastic tone of voice: ... *am I just supposed to change my thinking ,and everything will be right again?*

Culturally and cognitively, we are hard-wired to find meaning in the world and also to find solutions to problems. Yet when these solutions appear to be too simple or too easy, the logical and sceptical part of our brain kicks- n, and we consider them as being naive or too simplistic. But that is epreciselywhat I am asking you to do! Release the logical mind for a while and let your intuitive or instinctive part of your reasoning take the helm; or at least until you have completed reading this book.

Generally, we see our truth as being ultimately ... true. Our experience of our trealityis just the conglomeration of past thoughts which all go toward making our beliefs about this or that. However, perhaps our thoughts and beliefs have jonlybeen a mirage of reality ,and maybe it is time to remove the emojis from the gauges and take a second or third look at our *now* reality.

You have not listened to the warning calls ,and now you are experiencing significant pain or negative emotions. Your perfectionism has probably reduced your list of doable actions down to perhaps one or two possible things. Are you confusing your loyalty to the company with your lcommitmentto yourself? And, more importantly, can you be csurethat, when push comes to shove, your company is 100% loyal to you, your wellbeing and your future? This sunk cost loyalty in the time that you have invested in your company has provided you with experience, together with the financial rewards each month for working there. Although you have invested your time in that company, consider this sunk cost investment, similar to inadvertently hiring a car on holiday without a possible refund. Now you can either use the car or not (as you have paid for it). However, if you use the car, without enjoying the process, then you are continuing on with the negative first mistake by adding a further merrorto the original one, rather than sitting by the pool and drinking a Pina Colada in the sun.

At the start of the 1st Industrial Revolution people were summoned from the countryside to come, live and work in the big cities so that they were in a convenient vicinity to the factory and become part of a united paid workforce. Then, after leaving the factory or workplace, they were virtually 'free' to live their lives and do anything else that they wanted to do.

Conversely, now being on the cusp of the 4th Industrial Revolution, we are now seeing the gradual movement away from the ntypicaloffice environment, uprooted from the confines of a modern 'supposedly social' open-plan office design. Arguably, mcurrentworking practices mean that we are now more empowered by the new working contracts, together with the technological advances, such as: home office, remote working, mobile adaptability, digitalisation, etc.

However, this so-called freedom that we are now witnessing,has been questioned and debated in recent times. There is ncurrentlyan ever -ncreasing blurring of the work/leisure boundaries, highlighting the dangers and problems of being mentally 'at work', even when we are in fact physically away from the working environment. This is especially true for a new class of people, the working poor, those who despite working, still do not earn enough to live and survive on, together with them lacking the ncommon erms and benefits of a fixed-term contract (such as: holiday pay, regular income, sick-leave, etc.).

There have been a plethora of other books about this subject, but most have not touched on a holistic approach to work, working and being employed. It is now widely observed and reported that global companies and corporations, although being held responsible for their employees with rules, regulations and laws, they are not inherently interested in increasing the well-being of the population, the state or society, but rsomewhatsolely concerned with increasing the profits for their investors and shareholders.

Historically, it is icrucialthat both the elder and younger employees understand and respect the diverse point in time and attitudes of the other. The older colleague is trying to fathom out the work ethic of the young internee; similarly , he younger employee can not quite get its head around the older colleague regarding loyalty and tradition.

Recent studies have shown, that having intergenerational working solidarity, together with collective intelligence, happening within the same organisation or company, that there is a unique bonding between the different generations and this is generally regarded as beneficial for the over ll working environment and atmosphere of the company. This bonding not only incorporates trealunderstanding, support and solidarity, but it also fosters a closeness between colleagues or members of the workforce from different generations, which can, not only lead to a helping environment, ut also helps to make the organisation run more smoothly and more efficiently, as well.

This "generational observing" and "collective intelligence" have now both, not only become paramount in understanding and finding meaning in the attitudes of their opposites, but it is also important in observational learning, linked to self-efficacy (the ability to the way we look at goals, tasks, etc.). Sharing this collective or group intelligence grows from the collaboration and collective effort, especially when decision-making and cohesion needsto happen within an organisation or company. For this reason, and for the interests of both parties, understanding and respecting someone else's point of view becomes mutually beneficial.

To fully comprehend and possibly accept the norms of the past; and compare these to the values and differences of present -ay employment, such as the notion of presenteeism (going to work, despite feeling or being ill), increases the general understanding of the other and acts to remove potential boundaries and obstacles from all interpersonal relationships at work.

When we trust or bond with our elected government or the companies who provide us with their goods and services, we expect a certain amount of trust and truth. When this truth gets distorted ,and untruths are being expounded ,we need someone bmore significantthan ourselves to fight for our rights and empowerment.

The power of the trade union movement, actively fighting for workers' rights and empowerment, together with the collective bargaining of the 1960s and '70s, has been slowly decimated over the years by successive governments through law changes and the ideological use of the media. However, since the 1980s, and after the fallout of the world market banking crash of 2007-8, neoliberalism has become and remains in some form the predominant economic and governmental force in most modern western countries.

Neoliberalism, on the face of it, seems like a successful economic philosophy, which strives to propagate and embrace the concept of the free market. Although many see it as a harsh and brutal efinancialsystem, which helps to mask the disempowerment of the workers, and, at the same time, protecting the group at the top (the 1% that own 90% of everything), neoliberalism, nevertheless enjoys, celebrates and promotes the privatisation of state-run/state-owned public utilities and services, while, at the same time, encourages unfettered competition whenever and wherever possible, which however, more importantly, infringes upon the empowerment of the employees who work in these organisations and companies.

As mentioned before, social activists and political critics have criticised neoliberalism for helping to mask and protect the advantaged group at the top of society - those that own 90% of everything - i.e. big businesses and large corporations. Together with its harsh use and adoption of extreme austerity measures, such as legislating and implementing cuts in welfare for the poorest in society (those unable to work or have been deemed "fit for work" such as the disabled and those with progressive diseases and mental illnesses, etc.); or the working poor (those in the GIG or Agile economies); and this has led to a significant long-term increase in stress when considering leaving or changing a "bad" or stressful job voluntarily.

Similar to modern businesses and organisations, these neoliberalist governments have also made significant changes to employment laws and regulations. These have also been questioned and criticised by many leading academics and NGOs,;however, Neoliberalism remains the current, dominant economic and ideological force, trusting and relying heavily on self-control of business ethics, rather than the state regulation and control of things.

This, as a consequence, but especially for the employment of employees, has shown an increasing polarisation between those well-educated employees, those that are expected to work far more than the contractual hours agreed; and those less well-educated employees, those who are expected to work zero-hour contracts; irregular and unsocial hours; and whose contracts are insecure and offering low financial gain. Both, the well and less-educated employees, are experiencing many adverse side-effects of this new form of disempowerment, including extreme fatigue, insecurity and mental health issues, resulting in some employees trying temporarily to escape from this suffering with the misuse of alcohol, drugs and medication, among other things.

After we have learned a new skill ,we need to practice that skill until we become proficient at it. After a while, we "take on board" that skill, it becomes part of our skill-set, and is, for the most part, then just "taken for granted".

In a similar manner, the information in this book may appear somewhat naive to some, but in the words of Tracey Emin, when the critics were criticising her about her unmade bed: "... *anyone could present an unmade bed and call it art ...* ". Her honest and sharp response was: *"Well, **they didn't, did they?** No one had ever done that before."*

Which is my point, exactly!

Within the pages of the e-book there are highlighted "hyperlinks" where you can confirm the accuracy and validity of what I have written; together with finding out more about any of the diverse subject matter or interesting points covered.

And finally, this book offers a unique, holistic and historical insight and future vision into the changing ways we think about all aspects of our lives. Because you have not listened to the warning calls probably ,you have only one option open to you. And because of this, this book offers you a different way to look at your thoughts; your thought processes; and oprovidesdoable alternatives to once again take back control of your life.

Have a curious and inquiring mind; remain objective and rational; but also be kind to yourself throughout the pages.

This book is presented and should be read like two old loyal friends having an amicable chat, over a glass of wine, in front of an open fire, with smiles; slight disagreements; and interesting, but differing observations and points of view.

For this reason, and for the purpose of clarity, I will address you, the reader, throughout this book as "you", but just occasionally "he", "she", "we" or "us".

Introduction

"Burnout is nature's way of telling
you, you've been through the
motions but your soul has
departed; you're a zombie, a
member of the walking dead, a
sleepwalker. False optimism is like
administering stimulants to an
exhausted nervous system."
Sam Keen

A frequent and highly emotive topic of discussion within coaching in general and my business English sessions, in particular, are the topics of burnout and stress, in varying degrees of development, recognition and cognitive acceptance, of students and clients.

Some 30 or 40 years ago, it was generally regarded that the leading cause of mental illness, and having mental health problems, was intrinsically and solely linked to a chemical imbalance from within the brain.

This US-style medical model is now generally regarded as being outdated and far too simplistic. Modern research indicates that the root of depression emanates more from the environmental events and conditions, ultimately leading to stress, burnout and the things that eventually drive us mad, such as worry, anxiety and even suicidal thoughts.

Despite these modern findings, the pharmaceutical industry, together with the doctors, the media and the lobbyists, are still promoting medication, as a quick fix solution for basically every negative thing that happens to us in life (including mental illness), but also because there is big money to be made by selling their drugs to the populace.

The adverse effects of stress and burnout on the modern worker, and consequentially the company he or she works for, lingers on and plays havoc with every aspect of the organisation, but mainly its success and reputation.

However, when the student takes part in a training programme and enters the classroom, be it online or a face-to-face interaction, this offers a momentary release, an escape, a slight respite from the daily grind, comparable to an on/off switch; meditation; or time just being alone. Meditation is the easiest way of once again gaining that innate control of our lives. Research has shown that only 15 minutes of meditation, once a day, can significantly reduce stress. Yet, perhaps because of the bad press, spending time "reflecting" or "going inwards", is something that most people will still refuse to do.

We need to listen more closely to our inner being or intuition and to find a convincing excuse or reason to halt these circular and repeated patterns of negative thought. Searching for answers, to an unattainable solution, or using logic at these times of severe stress and worry, is not helpful or useful, because the mechanism behind our thoughts, via your mind, are corrupted, and as so, functioning inadequately and being mostly ineffective and undoubtedly unreliable. Also, most times when we are thinking, planning or deciding something in our minds we are, in fact worrying about things that may not actually be important or relevant at this exact time.

We need to put aside our learned, practised and traditional behaviour for a while; mainly because handling and dealing with struggle, stress and general problems in this way, is not going to help us in the long-term, plus there is very little chance of finding that convincing, peaceful answer we are ultimately looking for.

That boss, manager, colleague and those close to you, may condemn you at this time for trying out something new. They do not want you to find that easy short-cut to peace; nor to find that elusive "something" which paradoxically, they too are also desperately wanting and searching for themselves. Some might even consider or see this way of living as sinful - the sin of sloth; relinquishing your duties to others and generally appearing lazy and irresponsible.

Dealing with the pre- and post-stages of stress; apathy; being set unrealistic budgets, goals and deadlines; lack of recognition; expected loyalty and Continual Technological Connectivity (CTC); are all directly and indirectly responsible for, and related to, an employee's high levels of perceived stress, often resulting in symptoms, such as: sleeplessness, frustration, general irritability, plus varying degrees of physical and emotional pain.

As mentioned previously, empowerment can be seen as a double-edged sword. On the one hand, it offers flexibility and the chance for the employee to be more creative owing to advances in technology, allowing her now to work outside the traditional office environment. But on the other hand, empowerment has also led us down a foggy path ... muddying the borders between work and home life, and as so, has interfered with the standard, old-fashioned parameters of what is considered as having a "normal" and healthy work-life balance.

My own frustration at not being able to suggest immediate, adequate and practical strategies and solutions for my clients/students at these times of frustration and confusion, is the main reason for this book's publication; along with highlighting my own personal observations, research and findings; but also offering long-term solutions for the companies and organisations, as well.

If you are reading this book, regardless of your age or status within your organisation or company, and you have been signed off work by your doctor, then obviously it is a little late, but remain positive, for it is never too late to regain your balance. The ocean-liner, sailing boat or dingy has left the safety of the harbour and is now heading full-speed towards the open sea and to some unknown destination. The momentum gained since leaving the harbour is going to take a little longer to slow. However, it is not too late to return, taking back control of the helm once again, finding a harmonious and peaceful solution for our future, plus an adventurous next destination or new harbour to dock at. Nevertheless, we have to accept that boats are **not** made or designed to remain within the safety of the harbour walls. It is the *raison d'être* of ships and boats to sail out amongst the waves, tackling both stormy and calm weather in its stride and finally to experience and reach new and amazing places.

If you or your significant other are noticing 'signs' or 'inklings' that things at work, or even at home, are moving faster than you can comfortably control, then reading this book will undoubtedly give you a fresh and new mindset to help you take back control of your life, but also to gain a new perspective of the current situation in which you find yourself in. Having a fresh overview of the current situation may just be enough to avoid going over the top, or over the edge of the precipice.

Many of us in our professional lives, occasionally find ourselves in confusing and worrying situations; this is what I would like to call: "Situation X".

Just realise that being pushed, prodded, nudged, forced or propelled into taking on more than we can comfortably handle has led to this Situation X. The continual striving for an optimal and streamlined workplace, with little or no time to "switch off" during the day, because of the workload, together with the incessant forced connection to all the social media apps, all calling us for more and more connectivity, has inevitably led to a deterioration of our innate and precious personal well-being; and generally at the expense of our own psychological and physical health.

This modern trend of continuous and continual optimisation of the contemporary workplace, via qualitative management; large open space offices; total and uninterrupted connectivity; together with a striving for a more efficient and insatiable streamlining of the organisational process, is increasingly pushing the modern employee to breaking point.

"How far can we push him?"

"How heavy is the final straw to break her back?"

The arrival of this new modern norm, and the acceptance of this dystopian optimisation of all aspects of the workplace: time, place, interaction, is, in the opinion of many academics, not only tarnishing the image and reputation of the company; its clients and customers; but also having a long-term detrimental aefect with all those external connections related to that individual, outside work, nusuallythe close family, colleagues and friends.

Nevertheless, there is still a glimmer of hope on the horizon; even for those who are finding themselves in the "middle of nowhere" - in the middle of that 'dark stormy ocean' or in the midst of a solitary and excruciating painful place.

Although many in the business world might deem the explanations, conclusions and strategies in this book as being "simplistic" in nature and perhaps "unrealistic" in the modern business world, the majority of my clients, within the multitude of hierarchical structures, who have made significant and major changes to all areas of their lives, have found a marked improvement in their work/life/sleep/health/relationship balance. We now have the amarkedopportunity and ability to find our own unique balance. This book is here for those that want to revisit, return and find that healthy balance, and retrace back to that harmonious place once again.

Our past experiences have made us increasingly polarised in our thinking: black or white; right or wrong; bad or worse ways of doing something; etc. Before starting each of the chapters … just ponder, what happiness means to you?

Taking some quality "time out" for this life audit or to consider just "what we want", may be deemed a luxury, but it is not. It is probably the most important thing you can do at this stage. You will find that once you set aside some time for this process, strange, positively unique things, will start to happen and occur in your life. For example, while you are looking for something specific, you will find something else you were desperately looking for. This is called Serendipity (being in the right place at the right time). You will find that those coincidental thoughts,that you are experiencing in your dream or wake states,will suddenly start to "guide" and "empower" you. Consider these strange thoughts as signposts, from your unique, personal inner guide; assisting and encouraging you to find inner peace and satisfaction within your daily life … this is called Synchronicity.

Consider if you just want to deal with the symptoms of stress and burnout; or if you ware going t handle and use the more complicated preventative suggested measures laid out in this book?

Before describing and going through the following chapters of this book, I will hope and assume that your basic needs are being met; that your physiological needs, as Abraham Maslow described them, those fundamental things for a human being to survive, air, water and food, plus clothing, shelter and security are given and intact. If, however, you aackiin any of these, please seek immediate professional or voluntary help before setting out on the next llong eg of the journey to find your own unique pleasure, passion and purpose in life.

In **Chapter One** we will be discussing stress, depression and burnout, together with the **"hole"** that you have dug for yourself, symbolising your momentary life and circumstance. This time, however, without the usual blame, fear and embarrassment. We will be looking plainly and honestly at where you are now;,and your perception of the choices that are open to you and all modern employees (even if you tgenuinelybelieve or perceive that you have no areal options vailable at this present moment in time). The good news is, you always have choices, as Chapter Eight will later explain. Our mprimaryresponsibility and attention, in this chapter, is to ourselves (being totally selfish) and to "feel" for any possible options and opportunities that are open and available to us. We will, as much as possible, be avoiding the lrationalleft-brain thinking, as it has been this logical side of the brain, which has probably got us into this mess in the first place.

Chapter Two asks us to relax, and at the same time, consider if we are living too cognitively in the past or being too nostalgic in our present? Our acknowledgement, acceptance and place within our carefully sculptured lives (or holes) should be examined and perhaps exchanged by asking questions about possible other options open to us, such as: "Where you would like to be?" Even if we can ot epreciselysee or imagine a way of achieving that ideal place at present. Considering if **anything** and **everything** were possible: "What would you change?" or "What wouldn't you change?" The ability to look outside the box without fear and really listen to our own clarity of well-being instead of being numbed or deafened by it, s cundoubtedly eneficial and examined more within this chapter.

In **Chapter Three** we will explore the problems and our inability to say "no" when absolutely necessary; to distinguish between saying "no" and yet still foster company 'loyalty';,and believing that saying "no" can never mean "maybe". We will also look at the history and impact of age, culture, socialisation, class and gender issues, especially regarding deference and also the importance of setting clear boundaries. Also discussed, is the usefulness of having a voice in decision making; plus examining the gender pay gap; questioning authority; and being bloody-minded at work, as a form of rebellion and showing disdain.

Chapter Four considers when 'enough' really is 'enough'? We look again at our place in the world of work and home. What is and what is no longer irelevant What are we still willing to tolerate; and for how long? What happens when our best is still not enough to please the other people in our lives? Examined too, is the ever increasing demarcation of gender roles within society, together with the history of the working week, both being perhaps related to the reasons why we are now changing our jobs more frequently. By using the Stress Standardisation Scale ,we can evaluate our own level of stress, and then, if need be, take a break and ask ourselves new pertinent questions; then scrutinizs these answers to find our own truths. And not forgetting that, when we leave a job or career, we take our "complete selves" with us to the next place of work.

Chapter Five gets to grips with understanding the true nature and importance of momentum. By consciously considering the processes and benefits of slowing this momentum down, simply by just quietening the mind for a while (perhaps through meditation, movement or distraction) this can often offer us a unique pure path of guidance and ultimately doing things differently and more consciously. The chapter also discusses the significance of exchanging daily negative thoughts, in favour of those mubtle rand ereadily vailable positive ones, regardless if they appear somewhat counter-intuitive, counter-productive or naive on the surface. It is certainly not surprising that so many people are experiencing a stressful life and suffering burnout due to our increasingly hectic society. We will see that consciously questioning what we are doing and thinking about things is incredibly helpful and useful. We will be considering the amount of success we have had trying to find a solution to our problems, doing it the old- fashioned way; the way we were previously taught, regarding how to deal with conflictual pissues We will see that doing something new, interrupting our Zombie Routine, for no other reason other than wanting to do something differently, can be incredibly liberating, as seen in the 1970s series, Reginald Perrin.

Chapter Six, the largest chapter, examines the importance, relevance and our own need for change. Change, in itself, can either be seen as something positive or negative, depending on our stress levels; our involvement in its implementation; and our general acceptance and understanding of change when it occurs. This chapter examines the merits of accepting a holistic approach when dealing with all types of change, but especially intuitive change (things we "know" that will be beneficial for ourselves), together with those changes inflicted on us by other people.

As change is something natural ,we have to question why it is so feared by those at the bottom of the rung,and praised and venerated by those implementing the changes from the top. Let us explore the increasing dominance, influence and dangers of unnecessary change (change, for change sake and extreme optimisation of a process) within the top-down modern company or organisation. We will discover, too, the positive aspects of change, such as: questioning traditional and decadent thinking; preventing stagnation; and avoiding executives and the organisation as a whole, suffering from the Dinosaur Syndrome. We will analyse the history and usefulness of Change Management, as a method of planning, controlling and carrying out all necessary change. We will also be sifting through and questioning our beliefs and definitions regarding the words and phrases relating to the word **change**; investigating and scrutinising when change is healthy, good and right, such as when its foundations are serving us; and our own perceived perception of both negative and positive change in the modern workplace and the wider society.

We will be appraising the validity and usefulness of equating change with death, loyalty and truth; talking about the unhelpful hereditary baggage, as a learned response to change and decision-making, by dragging an outdated picture of the world (those taken for granted norms and values from previous generations) into the present moment. We will come to understand that all change must be seen in its broader sense, regardless of the sunken costs from the past, invested in doing it the old-fashioned way. Change should generally be seen as being beneficial for all parties, because of the experience and knowledge gained from the previous wmethodof doing something and, at the same time, it might also offer us a positive step forward into the future.

Finally, this chapter helps us to understand the principles of change and by accepting that change as a neutral concept; together with believing that going along with a change is just offering us a further stepping-stone towards our next chapter and future; and that we will never be completely satisfied or finished with something, even after reaching that future goal or achieving that change.

Chapter Seven asks us to embrace the journey towards our destiny more of the time; to enjoy the stepping-stones and the variety of the experience; and yet, at the same time, relish the actual moment more. Understand the importance of finding the right support and the acceptance of accepting necessary help from others. The chapter also offers seven tried and tested suggestions for self-care, touching on the following topics: sleep, mind-altering substances, exercise, spending, gambling, hydration, food and nutrition, and finally technology and other people.

Chapter Eight takes some of the theoretical issues from the previous chapters and offers practical and useful suggestions, regarding looking more into, for example: body weight, nutrition, water, keeping mentally active, mapping out working times and other things that might harm or help us. Together with the things that we take for granted, for example, the passing on of knowledge and keeping a positive vision of self. This chapter also reminds us to understand and take on board the ideas that, our lives are multifaceted in nature; and that the differing paths open to us at any time, are all ultimately leading to some place better; a life full of positive rendezvous'; and an adventurous destiny.

Chapter Nine examines the curious acceptance of struggle in modern society; it offers soothing words and tries to answer the lingering questions related to and regarding the issues raised in the previous chapters, such as: self-efficacy, empowerment, insomnia, dealing with grief and loss, the power of meditation, handling depression and being fully adaptable and flexible in stressful and at changeable times. It also explains and highlights the importance of being more egoititical. The chapter also encourages us to feel generally more free; free renough to be our own authentic selves; to know what we truly want; and to take time out to find our hidden desires; to find that certain 'something', our **raison d'être**, missing from our lives at this particular moment in time.

Meditation and mindfulness are examined and explained in easy terms in **Chapter Ten**. We look at the stigmatisation of meditation of the past and how, together with mindfulness, it is now praised and used in todern society to release stress and worry. We examine, too, the different types of meditation available, i.e. just walking and being out in nature; to prayer; to chanting; or doing Tai Chi;,and how mindfulness is now being used in both time and change management courses to alleviate stress in the workplace. We look at how to begin a meditation or mindfulness practise; the dos and don'ts; and the release of struggle when trying to quieten our minds. And finally, understanding and accepting that most negative thoughts and worries about the past, present and future are ultimately caused by our ccurrent orrupt chought practises and are perhaps not serving our own higher selves.

Chapter Eleven examines the importance and necessity of finding and living our passion; the acceptance and realisation that both 'bad' and 'good' things happen to us; and that all these things are just part of life … a fleeting dance between the past, the present and the future. In the chapter ,we also look at the new role of the coach, as more of a companion, rather than a bossy instructor. And by listing the 17 stages of the Hero's Journey, we can judge for ourselves, where we presently find ourselves - *departure, initiation* or *return*? The chapter also offers us the soothing idea that one never really misses an opportunity, because there ais flotilla of oorssibilities aiting to take us to our next port of call or adventure. The chapter concludes with our nfutureand immediate quest:

… to relax, to breathe and to feel more.

In this last chapter, we summarise the main points once again and ask pertinent questions regarding the future of carrying out this multi-pronged action plan and dealing with the many parts of our lives at the same time. The chapter also looks at and considers the positive and negative benefits of thought; deciding between our health and obligations to our work;

getting back on the wagon once again; believing that our true nature is incredibly forgiving; finding our passion and being passionate about what we do; and questioning why we dig giant holes in the first place - then jump into them, only to scramble out of them a short time after? **Chapter Twelve** also requires us to think more about the qualities of slowing down our minds and lives, which might mean avoiding digging those holes or having those problems in the first place.

As mentioned in Chapter Eleven, life is full of the ups and downs, however, most of the time, things are going pretty well for us ,and it is this contrast, described in this last chapter, which ultimately presents us with the spice and flavour of life. We now have to celebrate that new person more each morning; perhaps by writing down how we feel; what we are grateful for; and to never forget that things are not going to change until we cdecided to hange ourselves from within.

Nothing is more important than our own well-being and self-care. We only get one life ... so let us use it fully and to the best of our ability.

**"Whoosh!
What was that?
That was your life, mate!
That was quick ... do I get another?
Sorry, mate ... that's your lot."**
*Basil Fawlty
(Fawlty Towers)*

Whilseliving in London, a famous painter once told and reminded me that:

"You are a long time dead!"

... suevidentlyeaning, that our lives are far too short and
imessential waste; too short not to take thoughtful action and
enjoy life to the fullest; too short for struggle; too short to be
stressed with unimportant things and people. We apparently
have forgotten that life is, and should always be treated and
lived as, a balanced adventure; full of excitement and creative
challenges; joyful for the most part and full of ease, happiness,
contentment and pleasure.

EvEvenf you do not make it to the end of this book, always
remember to spend more time outside in nature, pamper
yourself more and smile more broadly. EvAlso,f you have lost
everything in your material world know in your heart that this
pain will not last forever and this contrast is beneficial for your
further advancement. Know that soon, very soon indeed, you
will be back on your feet and speeding towards your next joyful
adventure.

Find out and know what you want; kealways ep this idea in
your mind's eye aspeak to your boss or manager. Explain where
you are; and where you want to be. Explain the momentary
facts, as you see them and describe your feelings, ecause y, ur
feelings can nt be questioned or negated; they are your property,
use them well. If after all this honesty and explanation your
boss or manager still does not want to help you or can nt hear
you; you basically have to then consider, if you really want to
continue working for this company? Or if you should 'move

on' to your next challenge and point of call upon your itinerary. Most likely, making this step to part with your present company is filled with anticipation, trepidation and angst, but this is a step that you can be proud of when you look back at this decision later on and in introspection.

This book will offer many analogies and metaphors, all are readable but, depending on where you are, physically, situationally and emotionally, you may not actually 'hear' everything or what is being explained or iterated.

This book is going to hopefully present a new way of being in the world and in ana naturalay that you are going to hear it. You might be familiar with some of the themes and topics presented, for this I, apologise in advance. Similarly, we take so many things for granted; we might know something "intellectually" or "theoretically", but to really knunderstand something ntimately" we have to use that knowledge daily by putting it into our practices and daily routines.

Know that you probably can nt change the circumstances and situations regarding what is happening to you at this present moment; know, too, that you can nt easily change the words, actions and intentions of other people; and know that the only sure thing which you have control over is …

… the way you think!

Let go of the notion that we are alone; even if you feel that way occasionally. Know that we are part of something much bigger; connected and never walking alone. Negative emotions are just an indicator telling us, that our inner self does not agree with these negative thoughts - that is why they are so painful.

Be more trusting and finally, know that you are on YOUR

path. This path is unique and belongs only to you and no one else. Accept, too, that this path, hwhichou are treading on, s good, right and leading you to many new and exciting future places; even if you can nt see or feel them at the moment.

1

WHERE ARE YOU NOW?

"The unexamined life
is not worth living."
Socrates

So, as mentioned previously in the introduction, it is of the utmost importance to take stock and find out exactly where we are ... now – right at this moment in time. Consider less about the material and logical things and concentrate more on those visceral things - emotions, feelings and *knowings*.

However, the most important thing to remember in this chapter is ... we have to be happy with where we are at this moment in time; no matter how bad things might look or feel. The first working title of this chapter was to be: **Selfishness**. Being selfish and thinking more about our own well-being, is absolutely necessary when we are overwhelmed with stress, anxiety and worry; so that we can find a "better" and yet "different" perspective to help us rebalance, take stock, examine our whole selves and where we currently are.

Bad things or life situations do not generally happen overnight. This has probably been building up for some time now, and you chose not to deal with those things which were affecting or annoying you. Now, this life situation has your full attention. The options once available in the past are probably no longer there or even usable. This is to get you to concentrate on what is; what is essential?; what is now paramount?; and how you can ultimately progress and move on. The trick here is that we have to be happy and contented with where we are today ... at this very moment. To give up the struggle of finding an immediate and logical conclusion and give up trying to find a permanent solution to an ongoing problem or circumstance. The only sure thing we can do is to surrender to the silence for a short while; relax; breathe, and just let the dust settle.

Later on, in Chapter Five, we are going to be looking at the concept of momentum more closely, however, just for now, realise that in order for us to start moving in an opposite but positive direction, we need to first "slow down" and stop, before significant change is doable or achievable.

We have the choice to change our thinking either now or later. Our inner guide or intuitive nature is incredibly tolerant and patient with us; and will just wait for us to inevitably move once again in a positive direction. If you are now feeling frustrated because of this, know that our decisions or indecisions are both good and natural. The most important thing to remember is that when we make real decisions, we should always have a positive attitude to balance ourselves with. Consider if this path is still something that you wish to continue upon? Or have the most important things now changed? Consider the pit

2

that you have dug for yourself, undoubtedly symbolic of your life in general. Realise that, although we can all decorate our unique holes; and surround ourselves with all the trappings of success; i.e. attractive people, objects, money, wealth, etc.; we still, however, feel restricted and controlled. And, if push comes to shove, we are still in a self-dug hole in the ground, which might be limiting our movement; view of the future; further expansion; and, ultimately, our future freedom.

By relaxing more, taking a little more time to do a bit of reconnaissance and to address the situation head-on, might be more time consuming and even a little frightening, however, it is undoubtedly worth every hair-raising moment and should not be ignored, missed or for that matter, taken for granted.

When describing your moment in time, do not, like many others, make it worse than it actually is, but again, understand and define your current situation, using as much detail as possible.

Imagine being given a new project to project manage; you are still in the planning stage: deadline, budget, team to be sorted later, but again it is your responsibility to write a well-thought-out plan or agenda for the project as a whole. Take this stage seriously; for what is more important, than your life and your well-being?

Also, write from the heart and express those momentary emotions. You might find searching for these emotions hard to find once again, after such a long time of hiding them away from other people and perhaps even yourself. Consider how are you really feeling? What is your dominant emotion? Imagine waking up at 03:13 in the middle of the night. What are your thoughts? How are you feeling? Tucked up nicely and enjoying your comfy bed? Or thinking about the problems of that project

3

or colleague at work?

Also, list any physical effects which are affecting you in all areas of your life. The holistic you is all part of your whole self, which is immensely important for the second part of the process, and to be worked on and continued in the next chapter.

Probably there are only going to be two actual and credible scenarios at this moment in time:

a) You find yourself in an awkward situation where you are experiencing some sort of 'hard to express' constant discomfort. Resulting in that you wish you had more time to wind down and relax, a seemingly rare commodity recently, and to find a solution, but ...

i) You don't even know if there are any real do-able solutions, which all seem to be leading down a one-way negative street towards helplessness, anxiety and a general feeling of fatalism.

ii) And, if there are any solutions to Situation X, you certainly cannot see them through the fog of the constant and incessant activity, heavy workload and perhaps that striving for perfection at work.

b) The alarm is ringing, but even more disturbing than the sirens, you seem to be the only one hearing these loud and incessant bells and whistles. You know that something is wrong and *instinctively* you feel and understand that this is not how things are supposed to be. Perhaps a colleague has suddenly disappeared from the workplace; rumours have it, that she has burnt the candle at both ends for too long now and has the **Big B**. Her absence means that you are now expected, directly and indirectly, to take over her responsibilities, on top of your own expected workload.

In *"**Nineteen Eighty-Four**"*, a dystopian novel by George Orwell, he describes a society which has ultimate control over the population mainly by intimidation but also controlled through the media. The population are subjected to an inescapable and continual form of brainwashing through this propaganda, and this is used to control and suppress the society as a whole.

One of the main paradoxical slogans used throughout the book is: "Ignorance is Strength", which was part of the central ideological concept called: Doublethink (having two contradictory thoughts at the same time and believing both). Although written in 1949, Orwell perfectly describes our present inability and struggle to detach ourselves from both social media, but also the media in general.

Working in a top-down organisation; accepting other people's truths; and together with the feelings and emotions of powerlessness and the ever-increasing monotonous working practises; we can draw essential similarities between the Doublethink (a state of mind having inconsistent thoughts, beliefs and attitudes) of the novel and the cognitive dissonance of today's modern working philosophies.

For are we now just expected to accept and believe that by taking on and allowing more work, together with these new working practices, this somehow necessary and good; regardless of the potential damage to our own well-being and ignoring our own health concerns by doing this? By continuing to work, despite knowing and feeling out of control and being overwhelmed, some employees feel intimidated and refuse to make necessary changes, because they believe that failure to abide by these subtle expectations can lead to them being labelled as "inferior" or even "disloyal" in the eyes of their colleagues and bosses.

Perhaps you can still hear the strangely awkward and hesitant voice of your boss at the Christmas dinner asking all those

assembled to:
- do more;
- be even more efficient;
- to waste less time and money;
- to pull together towards the company's mission statement;
- on and on;
- more of the same;
- *ad infineitem.*

Despite this, there was also strangely no mention about any collateral damage that has taken place; or of the recent consequences which these expectations have caused; and to whom. And even more curious was that there was little or no mention regarding the amount of negative atmosphere now within the firm, owing to this ongoing stress; or what long-term consequences will this have on the company; its employees; its reputation in the business world; with its competitors; and ultimately, the crucial profits needed to succeed and survive.

We are looking more now towards a new holistic approach to the current situation. Something more intuitive and ... **right**; so intuitively right, in fact, that there is no, or very little, *contra* when we are thinking or talking about this possible or probable change happening. We usually escape this utopian idea, or holistic middle ground, with excuses such as:

a) I had a rough day, week or month
b) My partner left me
c) My boyfriend slept with that bitch
d) If you had the level of stress that I have ...
e) I have no time to change
f) I have no willpower to change

Task No. 1

Start by writing an honest review of your life. Now, right now, and at this exact moment! Take some time off - personal time - to write a very personal life audit, describing with a few but honest paragraphs, about your current situation. Pull over in the car; switch off your phone; hide in the loo; phone in sick; do anything you can, to take yourself away from your current environment just for a moment in time. Imagine talking to an old and trusted friend. Explain by writing down the feelings and emotions which you are experiencing regarding the current situation; together with the long unwritten list of excuses for not doing what needs to be done. Lastly, write down any physical or mental health issues that you are currently experiencing and then prioritise them.

Similar to alcoholism and obesity, burnout and stress creep up on us, like a crouching lion on the *qui vive* in the darkness. What started out with just a glass of wine or a beer with colleagues after work; or that large quick burger and French fries at lunchtime; has not only developed into a serious drinking problem; or bulging waistlines, with high levels of cholesterol; but has now become an essential and significant part of our daily routine; and now begrudgingly accepted as usual. We arrive at the harbour 'needing' the alcohol and the fast food to get us through the day, and even more scary, we now "use" these things as laudable excuses to celebrate "a job well done".

This double-edged killer has not been adequately addressed or truly researched and especially not in the modern, state-of-the-art workplace. In this current age of "extreme quality management" and "optimisation of process"; with its hectic schedules, together with the employees who are expected to work efficiently and attentively there; there seems to lack real understanding of reality and an empathetic realisation that we fluctuate like the sine curve - the ups and downs of life; energy; inspiration, etc. This *'pull up your socks'* and the *'I can ...'* spirit, are still being promoted and more so even expected now; but especially in the financial and service sectors, and noticeably amongst the more inexperienced and younger internees.

<u>Truth No.1</u>
Know that you are Perfect - no matter what anyone else might say or think!

2

WHERE WOULD YOU LIKE TO BE?

"I know where I'm going and I know the truth, and I don't have to be what you want me to be. I'm free to be what I want."

Muhammad Ali

Do you remember the last time you ate the best chocolate cake, ever? We are so prone to get nostalgic with our memories of the past, that often we now believe that in the future we will never eat cake like that again. Know that, regardless of how great that chocolate cake was, the next one will be even better … even perhaps ten times better.

It is too easy to think back to bye-gone days and feel that emotional and intense loss, intertwined with having things change over time, and remember that all this is quite normal. In a similar way to the cake, we just have to believe that the

9

future is bright and that good things are coming. There is no need to panic, just breathe and know that things are just playing out their natural course and things can only get better.

Now that you have hopefully completed your detailed report about yourself, and having taken into consideration most if not all of the issues that might have crept up on you over time, it is now time to consider … where you would prefer to be? And who would you prefer to be?

You have dug a giant deep hole for yourself. Despite it being dark and dank, you have recently and over time purposely thrown yourself into it, but now trying to find suitable and possible ways of escaping out of it. Being kind to yourself is key here, this self-kindness is the way you would treat a loved one; someone who you cared a lot about; or even perhaps a loyal key account client or customer.

We are not talking about some idealised image of yourself, certainly not the images from the adverts on TV or social media, but an authentic image of yourself being free, comfortable and full of that natural, glowing energy. This "ideal image" might be anything from having more peace of mind in general, to having a positive attitude towards a specific aspect of your life.

Taking immediate action is an integral part of allowing for this dynamic change to take place. 'Knowing Something' is one thing, but actually using that knowledge and doing something to achieve change takes courage, time, steadfastness and a willingness to look at your life from a totally different perspective.

With this newly completed report, your report about Situation X, containing your feelings, fears and any physical or mental health issues, you are now armed with a qualified and logical list of where you think you are. Our perception of where we think we are, is immensely important, even significantly more important than the perceived reality of others close to us. This personalised perspective highlights our emotional stability or instability and this realisation can be a great indicator of what needs to be done, when and with whom.

Before we begin to put this new structure in place, we first need to get into the right frame of mind (body and spirit both come later on within the chapters). To do this, take yourself away from everyone else. Find a quiet place where you will not be disturbed. Switch off your mobile phone or cell and just be in the moment. Your mind-chatter will most likely be turbulent and chaotic, do not worry about this, this is quite normal and must be expected.

Think back to some memory of the past in which you felt safe and secure. Perhaps a positive childhood memory or of a place where you can easily remember and bring to the fore. This might also take a little time; however, this step is not only really significant but will give you a secure place to allow the possibility to consider new things. You are going to use this memory or memories in the future when the negative thoughts return, as they certainly will. That is all part of being a conscious human being and living in a chaotic and hectic society. Once you have at least one memory, then write this down on a piece of paper, using only a few words or phrases which can symbolise this happy and safe time.

<u>Task No.2</u>

Now write the following words on another piece of paper:
LOVE, PEACE, QUIET, EASE, SECURE, ENJOY, FUN.

Now consider for a few moments what each of these words means to you ... there are no right or wrong answers. Do not wait for inspiration before doing this ... every time your mind begins to wander ... come back to that good-feeling, positive thought from the past. Now take each word in the order it is written and write a sentence or two about what each of these words means to you. This could be a memory, a dream, a person, an event, an emotion, etc. nothing is wrong. Once you have completed this ta,sk continuon e with the next part.

LOVE

Love ... a strong feeling of affection and sexual attraction for someone.

fondness, tenderness, warmth, intimacy,
attachment, endearment, devotion,
adoration,doting, idolisation, worship,
passion, ardour, desire,lust, yearning,
infatuation, adulation, besottedness,
compassion, care, caring, regard, solicitude,
concern, warmth, friendliness, friendship,
kindness, charity, goodwill, sympathy,
kindliness, altruism, philanthropy,
unselfishness, benevolence, brotherliness,
sisterliness, fellow feeling, humanity,
relationship, love affair,affair, romance,
liaison, affair of the heart, intrigue, amour ...

(c) Coach Antony

Although it might not seem it, here comes the fun part of the whole process ... considering what would be:

... the best thing possible that could happen to you now?

It is all well and good knowing where you are, but much more important is to know where you would rather be. Not caring where you would rather be, anywhere else but here, is not specific enough.

Task No. 3

Throw rationality out of the window for the next few hours and allow yourself to brainstorm without restriction or hindrance; this is your opportunity to find ouprecisely y what you want and desire.

This might appear harder than it actually is. Not because it is actuallmore laboriouser, but more than likely, for so long now, you have put aside your own wishes, hopes and dreams for the future. If you find yourself drawing a blank at fir,st then the easiest thing to do is to write the opposite of everything that you have written in the previous chapter and then analyse and draw upon that.

Many of us have been raised/brought up/socialised /indoc-trinated to consider first the feelings of others. We were taught from an early age not to be egoistic; to always consider the feelings of others before that of our own; to put our own dreams on ho ; and basically be realistic **all** of the time. We have been struggling to hold our corks under the water, easy enough at the beginning, but becoming increasingly difficult as time and complexity goes on. Having said this, most have taken this ideal to an impossible and unrealistic place, a place in which it becomes increasingly hard to "return home" to regularal healthy place of egoism, self-worth and self-importance.

Those who travel a lot for business or pleasure, know that when the aircraft we are flying in, suffers a sudden cabin decompression, before helping others we need to fit and use our own oxygen mask, thus allowing us to remain conscious, and to then, if necessary, help others who might be having problems. With this in mind, and without the shame or guilt, we need to know right now what we want and need in our lives. For this to take place, we need time and a secure place to plan and prepare for this new situation.

Do not be surprised if you cn not come up with any new and creative ideas straightaway or even being able to think cohesive, clear or logical thoughts at the drop of a hat. You might want to return to those old, familiar negative thoughts, such as:

Why even bother?

What's the point?

What I want is unattainable, unrealistic and just wishful thinking.

… rather than what I am asking you to do, to remain positive and forwa-d lookingTherefore,hy it is important not to rush this step. This process should be given the exact same amount of thought and energy, equal to the previoumethodss in Chapter One. This process should also be treated with the same dignity, due diligence, importance and concentration as any project you are responsible for at work or in your company.

When examining and exploring the key benefits of brainstorming, perhaps allowing for that Eureka moment to finally come into existence, we permit the opportunity for new and alternative ideas to be born. Suddenly everything is opened up and allowed … and nothing is restricted or removed from the menu. To think outside the confines of a bx, generally gives us the unique potentiality to truly discover what is and what is not wanted any more.

The easiest wy, is to write down a few relevant sub-headings, such as **health, work, sleep, relationships, holiday times, salary, hobbies, travel destinations, relaxation, passions, etc.** and then expand these headings by writing a few sentences that truly describe what you would like to achieve in each of thoscriticalnt areas of your life. Remember that absolutely nothing is out of bounds or impossible – the sky is the limit.

Generally, we know instinctively, what is and what is no-

15

suitableod for us. The sad reality of modern life is that over ti,me we have become deafened or numbed to our intuitive "clarity of well-being". This is mainly due to our daily routine of struggle and now, always being in this survivalist mode, we are playing a dangerous game of Russian Roulette with our bodies and our thought processes. And, to make all this worse, this is happening on an indefinite loop, making clarity lesevidentus and visible, and meaning that change is now much harder to realise and fully achieve.

3

THE CHALLENGES OF SAYING NO!

"When you say no to the wrong people, it opens up the space for the right people to come in."
Joe Calloway

This chapter considers both the ongoing difficulty and effectiveness of, not only saying "no", but also really meaning "no", in our modern, fast moving and hectic society. To get what we want, it is incredibly important to be, not only assertive of our aims but at the same time, be able to set clear boundaries, to that boss, friend or loved one. This demarcates, not only some of the critical aspects of getting what we want or need in a relationship but more importantly, it also highlights our dependency and deference to others.

When being assertive or setting clear boundaries at work, it is

17

essential to look at and understand both the concepts of gender and class regarding our ease at saying: "no". The significance of socialisation, but especially for women, can be best summed up in the words of Simone de Beauvoir:

"One is not born, but rather becomes, a woman."
Simone de Beauvoir

Recent sociological, statistical and empirical research data shows that women are still struggling to say "no" more of the time (as seen in the sexual misconduct reporting in Hollywood of 2017-2018), but also setting clear boundaries in the home and at work. The World Economic Forum carried out research and found continuing evidence that women are being negatively affected by the gender pay gap and still lagging behind that of her male counterpart, despite the increase in the passing of governmental pay transparency legislation, such as that in Iceland in 2018. So the old-fashioned assigned traits of a woman expected to be "pretty, passive and heterosexual" still significantly affect her long-term life-chances; hopes and dreams of getting that promotion; and a comparable increase in salary.

This is perhaps due to learned cultural- and gender-related issues; an adopted and learned response from childhood and adolescence, mainly, but not solely, via the media, social media and other powerful institutions, remnants left over from a previous time and, ultimately, keeping and protecting the (male-dominated) status quo.

"In England women are still occasionally used instead of horses for hauling canal boats, because labour required to produce horses and machines is an accurately known quantity, while that required to maintain the woman of the surplus population is below all calculation."

Capital - Karl Marx (1860s)

https://en.wikiquote.org/wiki/Karl_Marx

Despite this, it is not only women who are now solely being affected by this disempowerment by working and being employed within the modern, environmentally stressful workplace.

Increasingly, more men are now also experiencing major debilitating stress and increasing levels of conflict at work; together with their apparent inability to confront and change these unrealistic and rigorous methods of working. They are also suffering and losing out when it comes to using practical negotiation skills; arguing a point, and even offering alternative suggestions within a brainstorming session. As a way of coping and surviving, both genders have developed subtle, yet powerful, strategies to avoid direct confrontation and saying "no" to other people, but especially those in power.

Some men, in the modern world, both privately, but also in the business world, have also become increasingly emasculated and significantly weakened over the decades, beginning with the onset of the sexual revolution of the 1960s.

These once clear, socially defined roles of men and women

have increasingly become blurred; bringing with it more confusion and hesitation for both sexes, and ultimately to the office environment and society as a whole. Some of the main reasons why we have such a problem saying "no" might be:

a) The fear of directly confronting the person doing the asking and questioning the hierarchy and authority of people above us.

b) Fear of receiving a bad or negative image; being seen as not helping in the joint struggle; or fear of the dominant team members when questioning their actions; and not pulling in the same direction as the majority, towards a common goal or the mission statement.

c) Fear of real and implicit consequences; for example: "... if you don't work the weekend, you won't get that expected promotion or next lucrative project."

d) Being seen or deemed as being too egoistic or arrogant, with exclusion from a group or team, as being the ultimate punishment.

In order for the socialisation process of children, in those formative years, to be genuinely effective and complete, it is paramount that the child abides by the societal expected norms and values of those major institutions in society. This teaching is done subtly through primary socialisation: the parents, siblings and other significant others within the home environment; and later, through secondary socialisation, where this continues via external institutions, such as the nursery, schools, clubs and associations, colleges/universities and, eventually, the workplace.

For a society to exist; be successful; continue and to thrive, there has to be a certain amount of adhesion in society to these written rules (laws and regulations); and those unwritten customs (cultural norms and values). In general, we learn and use these rules by subtle reward and punishment interaction directed towards us. What is and what is not deemed acceptable by those that control the dominant values of the society as a whole? These rules are perpetuated, mostly unconsciously, down through the generations, often without questioning their validity/necessity/fairness. Bigotry, racism, elitism and deference are all examples of negative forms of a continuation of these types of norms.

Bringing up and questioning "place and position" within an organisation may be seen as almost revolutionary and aggressive in nature. By examining outright the order and structure of a company (why are some less qualified people higher-up in the company and earning more); challenging the authority (acceptance or non-acceptance of the hierarchy and the confines and structure of management); and questioning tradition and the status quo (the importance of conserving traditions and non-change, by not rocking the boat too much), may lead to defensiveness and bewilderment from those at the top.

> *... just do what I say ... not what I do.*
> *... you are not paid to think ... but to do.*

Being told to do something without reason or blindly following orders from the top, generally just leads to an attitude of bloody-mindedness at work. Where we are secretly hoping that a change or something new will not be successful, proving you "right" and them "wrong"; regardless of any adverse personal or business effects on the company as a whole.

Similar to this bloody-mindedness work ethic, being excluded from the decision-making process, also generally disappoints, frustrates and saddens those without a voice. This wealth of unused resources, expertise, experience and input often leads to an employee feeling and experiencing disenfranchisement of the process and general negativity at work.

As mentioned before, Karl Marx (1818-1883) was convinced at that time, that revolution would happen in England rather than other countries because of the clear demarcation and defined class structure. Knowing and accepting your "place" within society, and ultimately your place in the structure of an organisation or company, (those employees above and below you) is paramount for its smooth running, its continuation and ultimately its own success.

The following black and white television sketch from the 1960s perfectly illustrates the subtle and accepted forms of class deference and class structure in British society of that time.

Two Ronnies Class Sketch: Cleese, Barker, and Corbett in the sketch as broadcast in April 1966 on YouTube.

Remarkably little has changed over the decades, other than an increase of the middle-classes, but this deference and acceptance remains in the hearts and minds of the British and American populations at large. People, now even more influenced by big business lobbyists and the media, are still somewhat fearful of looking at and confronting the high levels of inequality and the privileged classes.

An example of this might be seen by the indifference shown by the public, after the leaked Panama and Paradise Papers of 2015 and 2017. This is most likely the case because this destroys their perception of fairness; together with their own ability to have a real and active role in a fair society; and ultimately having fair and equal rules for all. So, remaining ignorant and disinterested in social and financial inequality stops them from questioning the unfairness of the society, otherwise, they would have to take a stance, become revolutionary and then to start to fight the corrupt system, together with its corrupt leaders.

When a young intern enters the business world, bright and fresh from school or university, and brimming with exciting and innovative new ideas, this might theoretically lead to a return of passion and inspiration within the company or organisation. However, these new ideas could, at the same time, begin to rock the boat, cause turbulence and changes to the status quo, together with also bringing with it stress and unease to those mature and traditional employees, those who have been in the company for a longer time.

With this in mind, we will be looking later at the positive effects of the interesting concept of "generational observing": the notion of mutual learning between the younger and older generations within the same workplace; together with the ideas, benefits and changes made by collective intelligence.

On a practical and authentic level, we need to, on the one hand, differentiate between just saying "no" to a request and being bloody-minded; but yet, at the same time: "be seen" as being helpful, wanting to help and to foster both company and team loyalty. So, by just saying "no" to a request, with only a two-second glance of total eye-to-eye contact is probably enough to make the point and show your determination; then, if need be, you can then give your positive reason why: *"I have to ..."*. Then, if necessary, and depending on the negative or neutral response, you can offer a possible alternative or compromise.

When not complying to a request, the first word out of your mouth should be ... No! This is something new for both parties, so do not be surprised when you awaken something new in the people who know you only as being a "yes-sayer". Expect confusion at first, together with anger, shock, disbelief from these Askers. This is something for you to practise, and then practise some more, until you become proficient at saying *no* with little or no guilt involved.

Expecting respect from others means expecting respect from yourself. This ultimately means, knowing and defining your boundaries clearly and accurately to all those concerned. You may be questioned or asked a second or third time because the Asker might think you have not fully understood the request or demand. Remain strong!

"No" really should always mean: "No!"

"No", should never mean, "Maybe!"

> *To illustrate this saying "no" and the idea of consent, examine this YouTube video and ask yourself ... are you sometimes being forced to drink tea? CONSENT - It's simple as tea. On YouTube*

4

WHEN ENOUGH, REALLY IS ENOUGH

"He who knows that enough is enough will always have enough."
Lao Tzu

Always remember, you can only do your best at any point in time. Realise and acknowledge that you are only human, and therefore, you cannot do more than your best. If your boss, manager or partner expects *more* than you can possibly do, then he or she is going to be deeply disappointed, but that is **not** really your problem. And sometimes, even after we have spent months doing something for someone else; perhaps causing sleepless nights; maybe working at the weekends; standing on our heads; doing an Irish jig; and singing *"Singin' in the Rain"* from the roof tops, this, still will not be enough for some people, but that is okay, too! Relax and acknowledge that you have done your best, and that is what counts in the end.

If you currently hate your job, before quitting and moving on to different pastures, it might be advisable to once again spend some quiet time or doing something else for a while and at a distance. After a few days or so … ask yourself the following question:

"How do I feel when I think about going back to work?"

Task Four:

Write your answer to this question below:

Now answer the following questions:

    a) Is the answer to the question really true?

    b) How do I know?

    c) Do I just need a more extended break?

    d) Think about some benefits of working there?

    e) Is it just the lack of recognition?

    f) If I could change only one thing … what would that one thing be?

    g) What would be the most significant disadvantage if I left?

    h) What are my chances of finding something more suitable at my age or level?

    i) What are the chances of a different type of job giving me more job satisfaction?

    j) Do others who work in the same sector have passion?

    k) Am I really being objective about this?

Writing in the 1930s, John Maynard Keynes, examined the history of the working week and speculated that the working week would eventually be reduced to about 15 hours, with employees deciding to spend their free time doing other things.

However, we frequently hear in the media about young internees, especially in the banking sector, who have died as a result of working extremely long hours, perhaps to impress their bosses or maybe to show a heightened form of dedication and loyalty to the company or department.

In this chapter, we will be discussing and evaluating the four different types or levels of stress. These can be categorised by using the **SSL** - "**Stress Standardisation Level**". Knowing at what level you are finding yourself, will be helpful later.

SSL
Stress Standardisation Level

- Level Zero Stress:
(medium-level stress, boredom, short-term contracts)
negative stress through inactivity, insecurity & exclusion.

- Level One Stress:
(low-level, short-term stress)
positive stress through challenges and variety.

- Level Two Stress:
(high-level stress, long-term, negative stress)
by having more to do than humanly possible.

- Level Three Stress:
(extremely high-levels of stress, over a long-term
negative and continuous stress resulting in
burnout & mental/physical illness or disease.

(c) Coach Antony
2018

The Stress Standardisation Level

Illustrating the **Level Zero**, Christian Bourion, a professor of social economics at Nancy Metz ICN Business School, suggests that in France, because of what he calls *"the restrictive labour laws"*, employees are experiencing "trauma", owing to theincreasing inactivity of the workplace. He suggests that his countrymen are "suffering" real psychological trauma as the result of this inactivity.

Similarly, Jean-Claude Delgènes, an expert in workplace health and safety, coined the term 'bore-out'. This happens when an employee is, among other things, excluded from the mainstream work activity, asked to do dull tasks, having little or no chance of promotion and not being directly involved in the working arena.

"We estimate that around 30 percent of the French workforce is bored with their jobs, but most stay because of their fear of unemployment."

Most employees would confirm that experiencing **Level One Stress** at work, on a daily basis, is generally the best place to be. It is a positive place where the mind is kept active and alert; where we have challenging and exciting tasks; and where we can manage our workload most of the time.

At the other end of the **SSL scale**, and between the years 2008 and 2009, 35 French employees from France Telecom shockingly took their own lives and which led to the former CEO of the company being placed under formal investigation, for psychological harassment of the workforce. Similarly, in 2014 another 8 deaths were reported at the same company, relating explicitly to working at the firm. Allegedly, the same CEO boasted that:

"I'll do it in one way or the other; by the window or by the door."

... and that he was determined to reduce the number of staff by 22,000. This was published in an internal company document from 2006 in Le Parisien, effectively to achieve *"greater efficiency"* after the privatisation two years before.

Moreover, the benefits of reducing the number of working hours, as suggested previously, can be compared to that of a recent working trial study in Sweden in 2015. This trial explored the concept of reducing the number of hours, for carers working shift-work, at a nursing home. An 8-hour working shift was reduced to that of a 6-hour shift, for the same salary, and two years later, this has resulted in an estimated 10% reduction in sick-leave, meaning that the nursing home had to spend less for agency staff; plus a perceived improvement in overall health of the employees by about 50%, compared to those who worked routine shift work contracts.

There comes a time in every relationship, business and private, when the only way forward is to tell the truth, and at the same time, be prepared to face the consequences of that said truth. In a marriage or long-term relationship, if something is found to be *missing*, appearing to have no more room for compromise or growth, then we need to be honest and address the elephant in the room. Similarly, in the work environment, the risk of saying "**no**" to people who have power over us, might mean that we might have to, in the short or long-term *"move on"*, even though this might increase our own level of stress and financial (in)security in the short-term.

In days gone by, not only were there more precise and defined demarcation of gender roles, as for example, regarding the upbringing or socialisation of children, but also the gender-specific allocation of jobs and assigned professions. This was, more than likely, assigned by what your mother or father did for a living; the education you received or did not receive; and connecting both previous points, the social class in which you lived in and experienced in your formative years. Previously, class, social and job mobility were extremely limited and hard to break out of, nevertheless, they were all intrinsically linked to one another; it was therefore the norm, for us to leave school, start a job and then remain there - in that job - until redundancy, retirement or death.

In the modern workplace, it is now more widely "acceptable", and perhaps even seen as being somewhat "positive", to change our job or move within a company to a new position on average every 3-5 years. These changes, appearing on an applicant's CV, *now* shows a new potential employer that the applicant is perhaps striving to *better themselves* and, at the same time, wanting to gain more experience, because of these frequent job changes; rather than, in the past, when this was deemed more as something "negative" showing the applicant's lack of loyalty, stability and steadfastness.

This once perceived stigma of "moving on" to greener fields is less likely to be seen or deemed as being treacherous or disloyal to the organisation anymore, even for those choosing a sideward movement within the same company.

To briefly reiterate, *a change is still a change.* However, something that was once seen as having negative connotations within the interview process has now turned into something more positive, seen more like a natural progression and having a positive attribute to employing someone. With this new way of thinking about change, consider now:

- Why you first started at your current place of employment?
- What has changed since that time?
- Remember how you felt being accepted?
- Think about one significant advantage of your current job/position?
- Are these changes more to do with the structure of the

company or the way you now perceive your place within the organisation?
- Just how bad are things at the moment?
- How long could you *"hold out"* and remain at your present job, if push-came-to-shove?
- And, consider carefully, if you could hold out in the short-term until you have, at least found, another suitable employment to tide you over?

Generally, spontaneously going out on a limb and leaving your position, without the financial support and security of having a steady income, will more than likely, *add* extra stress to the perceived pressure that you are having at this moment.

The future in general and our future, in particular, is uncertain in nature. No one can predict, with absolute certainty, what is going to happen next year, next week or even in the next ten minutes from now. Whereas change has certainly become faster moving and more inevitable in recent years, we still need to make alternative plans. However, we should always remember that no matter how much one's future plans, the future is always going to be an unknown path of surprises, something unexpected and hopefully exciting, but all ultimately leading to our own positive fate and personal destiny.

We should strive to remain positive when we are considering both the concept of change and the future. Both concepts offer a new place of being in the world; giving us hopeful and positive attributes, experiences and expectations.

Like in a game of chess, our lives and the unique decisions we make, highlight the many possible moves that we can make at any one time. The "ifs" and "thens" row of choices and sequences of events, help us to enjoy and complete the game, regardless if we win or lose.

So, we can either be shoved; gracefully pushed; or better still, decide to move on willingly by ourselves. When we decide and act on future plans, we need to, firstly, remain flexible in our approach; have a good over-view of the situation; avoid hesitation, because of lack of courage; not to struggle too much, because of our comfortable and convenient (decadent) lifestyles; and, lastly, avoid being a perfectionist all the time, waiting for everything to be *just right* before making changes and moving on.

Generally, one intuitively *knows* when things are **not** right, no matter how left-minded you think you are. Naturally, it is totally possible to just *wait and see*, pretending that things will change by themselves, but this is far too passive for most people and the momentum of things, that have happened before, all play a part in the dynamics of what is happening **now**.

If it helps, then, by all means, plan. Plan a strategy, but keep it simple and remain flexible and positive. Do not talk to too many people about your thoughts, ideas and plans. Keep them, for the most part, to yourself, or if you have the need to share, speak to someone *outside* your own working environment for the time being.

Ideally, when we have a few aces up our sleeves, we act more confidently, because we have a greater sense of negotiating and bargaining power. We appear more carefree and respond more positively to the outside world, subtly knowing that we cannot really lose at this point.

So, the trick, *if there is one trick available*, is to decide and consider when to draw the line and when to say those magical and liberating words:

Enough ... is Enough!!

However, if you choose to leave your current job and move on, before having done the necessary '*inner-work*', never forget, that you are taking "you", and your mindset, with you. More than likely those argumentative colleagues; that incompetent boss; that restrictive, claustrophobic, non-creative and negative workplace atmosphere; will follow; follow you in the guise of new argumentative colleagues, new incompetent bosses, etc. etc. to your next place of work.

These thought patterns and emotions are all tethered to your current way of "hyper-thinking"; not only yourself but other people; the amount of money you are now earning; how much money you think you actually need; your relationships; how confident you are; etc. etc.

5

UNDERSTANDING MOMENTUM

"Momentum is the bridge between a vision and its result."
Farshad Asl

As humans, we are in a constant and continual state of change, similar to that of the flow of a river (more about Change in Chapter Six). The flow of the river is constant, as is the real world outside our heads. While we are alive, there is a beautiful mix of movement, change and flow. This flow or momentum is symbolically linked to our thoughts and lives, and therefore, should be expected and even celebrated. Once momentum and velocity have begun, regardless if negative or positive, this process or state is impossible to suddenly halt and move in its opposite direction.

However, in stressful situations, our perception of the world (through thought) can be slowed by merely taking a step back and rebalancing ourselves, together with our thoughts. Through the process of daily meditation, we are more able to control our thoughts and significantly *slow the mind down* and, more importantly, find and use those "quiet gaps" between our thoughts when needed. (see Chapter Ten for more about Meditation).

Throughout this chapter, it is essential to realise, and honestly remember, that all our thoughts, both those positive and nagging serial negative thoughts, which repeatedly visit us in those moments between inactivity and our waking state, are just, but a snap of a stranger's fingers away from its opposite. Once we truly understand more about this "momentum of thought", it makes changing the direction of our thoughts, not exactly child's play, but significantly easier and kinder.

This section may at first appear counter-productive, counter-intuitive and somewhat naive, owing to how most of us have been socialised and educated about dealing with conflict and the general solving of problems. However, if you are still a little doubtful ... ***good***!! (see Chapter Twelve, later). But for the meantime, just consider:

- *- How much success have you recently had?*
- *- How much success have you had doing things in that familiar and traditional way – the way you have always dealt with such problems?*
- *- How much success have you had struggling to hold on to that truth eel?*

Now consider finally;

- *- How rational and objective can we be, living and working with insufficient sleep, ongoing stress and having an unhealthy lifestyle for long periods of time?*

Many years ago, there was an amazing advertisement for Sony, set on the hills of San Francisco and featuring 170,000 colourful bouncy balls. A perfect example of momentum and an ideal example of the problems of stopping or changing the direction of things once movement has been let loose.

Getting those camera shots and angles correct was paramount for the success of the video; as doing this again would be too time-consuming, complicated and costly. The director and camera people knew that once these balls were released from the top of the hills, there was no going back and there was no way that anyone could stop the momentum of these balls traversing down towards the bay.

Momentum is something so basic and taken for granted that sometimes we forget its usefulness and importance, especially when choosing a positive or negative vibration or thought at the start of the day. Like gravity, momentum is something which follows specific rules of physics. All objects remain still until the moment in which the object is set into motion by an outside force. Let us ponder if in the same way, our thoughts, moods, emotions, etc. are affected or influenced by the outside world when we leave a meditative or the sleep state?

Imagine starting your day off tomorrow in which you arrive at a train station having two platforms. Both platforms have identical trains waiting to head off in two different directions. The destination of each train is concealed and not evident. Which train would you take? As it seems to me, that there is no hard evidence or facts for you to make a "proper" decision, you are somewhat "forced" to rely on your intuition and gut feeling.

In the 1970s there was a British television programme called: *"The Fall and Rise of Reginald Perrin"* on YouTube.

This show tells the story of a middle-aged, middle manager who acts and thinks differently by the pointless nature of his job at an ice-cream factory. A truly perfect example of how we all deal with stress and burnout, together with bizarre examples of trying to make changes to a dull and predictable life.

We need to consciously stop, question and consider if what we are doing is taking us on a positive or negative momentum. This could be as easy as taking a different way to work? Or eating a different cereal for breakfast? Do something to interrupt your **Zombie Routine**. We need to reframe the old momentum by questioning almost everything that we now do, especially at the start of the day. After having done this for a few days, before getting up just lay there and think about something/one thing that you are grateful for. It might be the warmth of your bed or the comfy nature of the pillow. Then get up and continue to try to do something different or different from what you are used to.

The next morning, consider **TWO** things that you are grateful for; continue doing so for a further few days, adding to your list each morning. This is not going to be easy at the start, mainly because we have been playing the *same old, same old* song for so long now. However, after a week or so, you might begin to feel something different about yourself and your life; you might even hear positive comments coming from those that know you or those that are close.

You are distracting yourself from the old and limiting way of living your life and exchanging it with something new. In the beginning, it is perhaps only going to last for a few seconds or minutes, however, over time, these "good feeling" new thoughts will become increasingly dominant. You are reprogramming your old thought patterns and considering a deeper connection to your foundation and authentic self.

Your goal or aim is to exchange the old way of thinking, more and more each day. After a few weeks, you will find that old problems, and negative thoughts will resolve themselves automatically; giving you a somewhat *quieter* mind and consciousness. You have given up the struggle in return for trusting that you are now listening to your caring, authentic and intelligent autopilot or concierge who is caring and looking out for you.

You have been traditional and doing it the old fashion way for so long now, perhaps having shown little or no success. Now it is time to try something new for the next 7 days. Change your thinking and give yourself a break. Stop fighting yourself, in this fleeting and repeated arena of continual thought.

- - You have stopped listening to your feelings and the innate wisdom you were born with.
- - You have stopped listening to your heart, because generally if you just relax, you know "instinctively" what is right and what is wrong.
- - You have stopped listening to the needs and wants of having a healthy body.
- - You have concentrated too much of your energy and time on what others have told you about what success really is.

Embrace the contrast for a while; stop fighting the negative; and experiment by looking for the very best things in life; even from within those negative and depressing situations.

When you find this alignment, you are solution orientated, because without a problem there cannot be a solution. Become friendlier with the negative. Soothe yourself (see Chapter Nine later). Everything is good, perfect and evolving. Make peace with *what is* for a while!

"Find a place inside where there's joy, and the joy will burn out the pain."
Joseph Campbell

Do whatever you can, to get off the negative issue or subject in your life at present; that topic you know is doing you so much harm. Do not face the facts for a while! Do not worry about things or situations!

For a while, please do not think about those emotional and dominant things in your life, which you probably cannot change, at this particular moment, anyway.

6

CHANGE ... AND NOTHING ELSE MATTERS

**"Trust I seek and I find in you;
Every day for us something new;
Open mind for a different view;
And ... nothing else matters."**
Metallica

The primary purpose of this chapter, plus the overall philosophy behind this book, is to consider all aspects of decision-making and achieving doable and necessary change. Firstly, we should not panic when things change within our lives. Secondly, by listening to our own unique intuition, regarding possible ways of changing things, ultimately for our own betterment, we have the exclusive option to change this perceived way of thinking; and questioning and challenging this change, by the way this thought of change is heard in our own heads, regardless if it is being instigated by a boss, organisation, family member or even our own thoughts.

The word change means different things to different people. " ... to change for the better", generally means " ... an improvement" after an event. Similarly, " ... to change our ways", infers that something is perceived as "bad or negative" beforehand, this could be perhaps regarding some behaviour or emotion.

However, within this book, we shall be concentrating more on why some individuals within a company initiate change; change, for change sake; rather than, the necessity for change, itself. This can often be seen when a new executive wishes to leave his "mark" upon an organisation; or perhaps him wanting to implement some long-term change and therefore leaving a legacy after he has moved on.

Life, paradoxically, is inherently linked to death, together with our fear of illness, old age and general decline. Over the aeons, we have struggled to find meaning to life, and religion has helped many to come to terms with our finite bodies and lives, by promising us a life after death or some sort of reincarnation after the death experience.

Depending on the circumstance, the word change can be used in many ways - both positive and negative. "Change" - to make or become different; to exchange one thing for another thing, especially of a similar type; "Change our mind" to form a new opinion or make a original decision about something that is different from our old one; and "Change tack" to try something new or different but dealing with the same or similar problems. We often hear about "Change of scene"; a "Change agent" or "Agent of Change"; a person or group within an organisation whose job it is to work on a change programme to change an opinion or some sort of behaviour within a company.

We often hear the somewhat fatalistic expression; "... a

change is as good as a rest". Or someone being described as a "Champion of Change" being a person who is very keen or adamant of new or different ways of doing something, and is determined to make changes happen, regardless if liked or disliked. Having a "Change of Heart" about something, just means that one changes an opinion about someone or something.

All of these words, phrases, idioms and definitions are used to describe change in a multitude of areas and sectors, both in our private and professional lives. It is the meanings and emotions that we *assign* to each of these terms, which allows us to perceive something as being: "good", "neutral" or "bad".

So, being rational beings, we should understand and accept the inevitability of death; perhaps being the ultimate change. This end-station not only takes away our own power and influence but also reminds us that we are just mortal and fallible; leaving us vulnerable and even helpless. Depending on our ability to rationalise these thoughts, beliefs and fears, we have to transform and modify this inevitability of change, from an ending and something that is potentially life-threatening; to something novel which, while we are here, can instigate hope and perhaps promise us something new and exciting instead.

So being prepared and allowing for necessary change to take place, and, at the same time, consciously accepting and being an active part of that change, seems to be directly linked to achieving, not only our own happiness but also the benefits of enjoying a healthy mind, body and soul.

As previously mentioned, the period or length of grief after loss is dependent on one's acceptance, non-acceptance or denial of the change. Because all change is unique, what worked in the past is highly unlikely to work in the future, and a new strategy has to be carefully thought out and planned. For this, we need to have the feeling of security, enough time and a safe space to organise our thoughts, allowing us to consider a new and suitable strategy to move forward.

Nevertheless, without change or advancement, we risk becoming obsolete, bland and no longer competitive in the market. By not offering something new ... now, to our clients, customers and potential employers, we risk losing our own uniqueness and so our individual advantage. So, we need to find a perfect balance between change and stagnation; and always have a listening ear for new innovations; plus, the essential needs and wants of the people who we do business with or often come into contact with.

Failure to do this leads to an organisation experiencing the dinosaur syndrome. This syndrome is bathed in arrogance and invincibility by those at the top and often happens after a run of perceived success and decadence. The elite, or those with the power at the top of a company or organisation, wish that their own interests and places at the top will continue, together with the ongoing and recent successes of the company itself.

This is perhaps a result of some work ethic learned at an early age from a variety of different institutions. The central tenet taught or learned is that working "hard" is an important trait which builds character and should be considered as a virtue. Generally speaking, work should not be enjoyed, but rather something tolerated and accepted; and being the most important reason for your being in the world.

The sin of sloth (one of the seven deadly sins), the Protestant work ethic and some other religious work ideology teaches us that we are supposed to suffer in this life, trusting that only later we are going to live *the life of Reilly* in some afterlife or paradise.

So, accepting this belief that this lazy employee, although physically at work, is still not mentally pulling towards the ultimate good of the company, and does not really comprehend that all this new change taking place, is actually good for him or her to accept and buy in to.

This is perhaps the reason why we still consider suicide as a sin. The official wording to "commit suicide" has legal as well as religious and moral connotations. Living a miserably hard life in the past, perhaps not being able to provide for yourself and your family, meant that killing yourself would relieve this stress and burden. For this reason, suicide had to be prevented as a way to end this pain and escape this suffering. This suicidal ideation was frowned upon by the church, in collusion with the factory owners, because it meant the loss of an employee and disturbing the means of production.

Change Management is now big business. This concept, starting in the 1960s, looked at ways we can prepare for necessary change in an organisation, team or department. It originated from the various aspects, research and studies about grief or loss in our private lives, then overlays this on the world of business. This new perspective then strives to help change take place, finding a coherent and helpful business solution for all concerned.

The different Change Management methods are various and diverse, each using different concepts and starting points to help and support the entire organisation before, during and after change. The main idea is to redirect the allocated and given resources, i.e. the budget, the varying processes, the employees, the hierarchy, etc., to significantly change a company or organisation, and making it ultimately "better".

However, we will consider later, for whose betterment are these changes taking place?

A good change management model should consider all aspects of an organisation simultaneously, but especially the impact of all those being affected; the channels of communication between the affected areas, departments, employees, etc.; and finally, the timeline in which the said change should occur or be completed. However, as most employees are somewhat resistant and sceptical of swift and major change, the performance of the workforce may drop as a result. So, for example, when an organisation is faced with adopting a new technological advancement or innovation, training is typically expected and required. However, if this training is scheduled to be done parallel and in addition to the normal working day, this may cause friction and overwhelmment of the workforce.

Moreover, technological advances, the increase in social media and remote and mobile adaptability, together with these new working practises, have revolutionised all types of business; and the effect of this is an ever-increasing need for change, and therefore change management.

The whole company, together with its departments and employees, have to now learn, how to handle changes to the organisation and feel part of the control and continuous improvement of the change process.

Although many are critical of extreme change management, mainly due to the forced striving for an ever-increasing optimisation of a system or organisation, together with the kudos of the management and finally the questioning of the need for the initiation in the first place … "change, for change sake" is generally seen as not being helpful in the long run.

It is paramount that enough time should be invested in

looking at the current situation and to judge if the capability of the workforce to achieve the planned changes are both **realistic** and **doable**. As a leader, there should be a solid and united leadership image behind the change, and this should be clearly communicated, planned for and implemented; providing an effective strategy, especially preparing for and resolving any conflicts and/or perceived failures after the change has taken place.

Because of globalisation, and the increasing speed of communication, technology and the resource of knowledge, many companies are still concerned, even paranoid, that if they are not keeping up with other competitors, they will lose market share or influence with their customers or clients.

When a workforce is confronted with accepting this new change, their unwillingness to adapt has more to do with fear of all things new and anything that they are not familiar with, rather than the specific change itself. When things are moving too swiftly for an employee at the bottom of the hierarchy, he or she generally feels out of control and passive, because they seem to have less say in the decision-making process, together with having less time to act or react to these planned changes.

Change, once momentum has started, can be likened to birth and death, all inherently natural and normal and healthy for most of the people in society. This is regardless of whether you are living in a large modern city or on a tundra many miles from the nearest town or village. The quicker we can accept or buy-into this fact and really internalise it, the easier life gets.

There are two perceptive types of change – the positive and the negative. While we usually enjoy positive change when it occurs, we are often knocked off our feet when the opposite happens. However, change is neutral in its nature, and this should never be forgotten.

"Three things cannot be long hidden: the sun, the moon, and the truth" as the Buddha once said. Truth must be our long-term foundation, and it can only serve us, despite possibly causing probable, short-term and perceptual pain and suffering, in the present moment. Before starting a change process, we have to realise that there is a problem. The secret or our long-term goal has to be to "allow" things to occur, free of resistance, rather than with "force", via stress and worry, where we are trying in vain to "make" something "else" happen as a solution to a problem. This alignment or adherence to the value of truth equals our ability to really thrive and live a healthy, successful and happy life.

Generally, we consider and equate negative perceived change as having a lot of effort, attention and resistance to it. Even though it might not seem like it, but life ... *your life* ... is at its very best! You just cannot probably see it; know it; or feel it; at this present moment in time, because of the negative momentum that you have assigned to it. It is usual for things to happen to us; just as adjusting and rebalancing ourselves after a storm; and to eventually find our own equilibrium and rightness once again.

This perceived negative situation is generally only temporary and frequently just a stepping-stone from the next best thing. It might appear counter-intuitive, but (especially at the beginning) you might not see "exactly" where you are. More importantly, at this stage, is that you are looking forward and observing your future and where you are heading.

Realise that this nostalgic way of looking at and remembering the past - *those good old days* - does, in fact, do you a disservice.

If you make no comparisons with the past and accept that this new stepping-stone is potentially "something good", then you will set yourself free and gradually lose the learned resistance.

Change is constant and natural. Your willingness to embrace this concept of change; as is your ability to stabilise life's little wobbles; and be curious about the obstacles and problems along your path; are all key to your long-term emotional stability, progression and to achieve a healthy and natural peace of mind.

Accept, as much as possible, that we are never going to be completely satisfied or reach an ultimate goal or nirvana because there are no ultimate goals; only the next stepping-stone in front of us, and then, the one after that. For once we have arrived at a perceived "endpoint" or destination, we almost certainly search for further improvement and the next best thing to do. This is what being human is all about; developing our innate ability to improve, create and evolve.

Just because we have invested or sunk so much time, energy and money into a particular venture, job or career, perhaps we now need to reconsider if these sunken costs are currently working against us and our future happiness? We should ask ourselves the question:

"... am I working for the money or the satisfaction that I get from my work?"

Although top-down radical change might look and feel like a direct betrayal for a loyal and long-term employee at the bottom of the rung, those making the decisions at the top are also perhaps being forced to make similar transformative changes for themselves. They may also be concerned when leaving the security and familiarity of the harbour and venturing out into unchartered waters.

This feeling of significant loss, by experiencing the contrasting extremes of marriage/divorce, birth/death and employment/unemployment, brings to the fore, perceived or real emotional and hereditary existential angst. These issues have most likely been passed down to us or carried unconsciously along for the ride, like *hereditary baggage*, from our parents, grandparents and great-grandparents, etc. etc.

On a personal level and to recap, if we just change or alter our dietary needs in isolation, forgetting the other vital parts of our lives, such as exercise, sleep, relaxation, etc., it is not only going to make changing our diets and nutritional needs harder in the short-term, but also puts at risk the long-term prospects for overall success for the body as a whole.

We can consider change as either being what is happening from the inside (internal - what we are thinking and making happen) or from the outside (external - what is happening to us).

Again, depending on your state of mind, we are either in a place with a lot of effort, attention and resistance to the current situational change or we are accepting and allowing that change to take place, where there is a flow, an ease and a willing acceptance.

The importance of decision making, both in our personal and professional lives, is a significant part of accepting and being part of the change process. However, acknowledging the need to make a real decision might also lead to substantial problems and resistance related to and connected with other adjacent areas of our lives.

When change occurs in our lives, in society as a whole or in an organisation, there is always going to be the possibility that the change may not be as successful as initially thought out or planned.

If we simply exchange the way we look at change, for example: "curiosity of expectedness" rather than "striving for perfection", this small perceptive change of thought incorporates **ease** to the mix, rather than struggling to be "better" and more "effective" all of the time.

With this in mind, perhaps we should not only reward those who suggest and succeed in visible, positive change but also reward those who "dared to be different" and those that were courageous enough to "think outside the box". Because from these "good failures" we learn from the mistakes and experiences of trying something new and novel, despite not having succeeded in achieving the original aim of the change.

Rather than leaving a company because of this new and unwelcome change; or those who are planning to leave an organisation, either because they are approaching the age of retirement, or leaving the company to start somewhere else; we can sometimes use offered training or re-training courses to offset our frustration, rather than fighting against this impending change. Since most people do not have the stamina to fight against something in isolation or struggle for long periods of time, training offers us some respite from the change, together with actively learning something useful which is positive for general cognitive health and long-term well-being.

Once again, it all boils down to our perception of change, deciding for ourselves, if this is now a perceived or real "problem" or an actual or perceived "challenge"? This simple thought choice can make all the difference between enjoying the process of change or not.

7

STEPPING STONES AND SELF-CARE

"The past is a stepping-stone,
not a millstone."
Robert Plant

Previously we have discussed the crucial concepts of momentum and change. Let us now consider the present ... this present moment in time. This moment, *drum roll, please*, and every single moment is uniquely temporary and fleeting, and yet, depending on how we look at it, it is also empowering and challenging at the same time.

It is paramount to plan our future path, but at the same time remain flexible about the exact itineraries, plus having the ability to pause upon the next stepping-stone for balance, relaxation and contemplation of the journey already travelled. It is also essential to organise a certain amount of support and structure to assist us in obtaining guidance and aid for our own well-being. This chapter is divided into three parts and explains the most important aspects of building this holistic and self-supporting structure:

· Embracing the Journey
· Self-Care
· the Support of Others

EMBRACING THE JOURNEY

The analogy of a journey representing our lives is quite the perfect metaphor. It highlights the contrast when embarking upon a journey between struggle and ease; the winning and the losing; and the pain and the ecstasy. Upon every path there are many natural and unnatural, seen and hidden, obstacles before us; barriers that we need to either physically move, transverse or divert around if we are to move forward and progress upon our path.

Upon every journey, there are many symbolic hills, brooks, valleys, streams, mountains, rivers and oceans to cross or climb. Some are quiet, hypnotic and slow-moving; others are loud, aggressive and having rushing rapids to be wary of. We have to decide, at any given moment in time, if there is enough time and energy to enjoy, swim-in, traverse, wade-through and eventually perhaps even continue to cross or ascend the challengeable path or river before us.

You are crossing the stream via the stepping-stones beneath your feet. The secret, if there is a real secret to find, is to take your time; find your feet, find your balance and do not rush. Enjoy each stone and every experience. Find your stability on each and every stone and relish in its foundation and texture.

Each stone is nothing more than just a resting place in time.

Each stepping-stone is taking you further across the stream; your stream; which is, paradoxically transient, ever moving but never-ending. By stepping back and relaxing for a while, we have all that is needed to find our own balance, together with the opportunity and ability to secure a healthy counterbalance of emotion, consciousness and sleep. Together with this balance comes a pure holistic harmony, and this book is here for those that wish to find that place *once more* and to occasionally return there.

However, no one else can cross your stream; or trek your path; it is our destiny; our journey and something that is uniquely ours in nature. And, if this is the truth, we are ultimately and integrally responsible for our own progression. Celebrate and know that you are on your unique path, even though on some days this might not be too obvious or it being hard to see, being veiled in thick, dank and impenetrable fog. Accept, also, that you have always been on your path; even when, in the past, those perceived negative things happened to you; those things that were questionable; or something that appeared or changed in your life that you did not wish for or even want.

We are ALL fallible and fearful at times. Facing up to this fallibility and fear, causing emotions such as shame, guilt and embarrassment, takes courage and yet, at the same time, shows our vulnerable and human side. We have good days and bad days, with life being a continual roller-coaster, with its ups and downs; this is normal, this is how it is and will undoubtedly continue to be in the future.

So, what someone else sees as being successful or being a failure in life (be it a colleague, boss, partner or parent) should not dishearten or negatively influence us; just as a non-directive coach should generally not make decisions for his or her client.

The good news is, that we cannot stray far from our own intended paths; as it is ongoing, full of exciting experiences, leading to strange and curious adventures and ultimately, never-ending. The interaction with others, experiencing the good and the bad times, only adds contrast and spice to the mix, which in turn, tests our agility, ability and assiduity at each throw of the dice.

Each major event that we encounter, just adds colour, texture and melody to this up-to-this-moment person you have become. For, we are not the same person as we were yesterday. We are a work in progress! A transitional working title. Each challenge encountered transforms and strengthens our inner being. Each smile from a stranger; each chance meeting; each thought confirms that we are going the right way. For these smiles, chance meetings and good-feeling thoughts, all originated from our deeper consciousness and are just signposts that we are about to start a new leg of the journey.

YOUR SUPPORT STRUCTURE

We are looking to get a healthy support system in place, to assist us, if and when needed. Just knowing that someone is there for us, our life-raft or safety harness, if you like, can mean the difference between the warm feeling of success and/or the perceived cold feeling of failure. However, as discussed further on in this chapter, there are no real failures in life; just an ongoing string of learning experiences.

Being honest with someone, in times of change, generally helps us to identify the true problem quicker. It can also assist in hearing what we are saying and, at the same time, question the logic or unreasonableness behind our thoughts and our general mode of thinking. We take so many things for granted, and a good confidant is just one of those things. If you do not have someone to listen to you presently, then try to find someone who you feel will be patient and empathetic to listen to you objectively.

When we are explaining "our story" to that trusted one, we will hear our own problems and arguments and either they will sound *authentic* or *false*. If they seem authentic, then we know that there is a majority of truth behind what we are saying; alternatively, if we hear ourselves speaking, but do not believe what we are saying, then we know intuitively that we need more time to consider something else, reassess or re-plan.

Our goal now is to get enough people on our side, having a few good, reliable team members to rally-around and encourage us, if and when things start to get tough. Consider why, when we are struggling with life's little problems, perhaps those things that we have no passion or inclination in doing, we cannot delegate this thing to someone else. If, for example, we are not interested in figures, bureaucracy and taxes, why then, should we do our own tax returns? There are plenty of people out there that are really happy and willing to do these things for us. Practise and learn how to delegate and how to share the load or burden more.

SELF-CARE

You have hopefully put some sort of support structure into place, to assist you in this new unfolding process. You may have already noticed small, but significant changes, that have taken place in just this pre-operational step.

57

Remember, that what we have covered so far in this book is going to be a gradual, long-term, multi-pronged process, helping you to return to a more holistic and peaceful place, and where you will be encountering and understanding more about an instinctual "rightness" to all decision-making and taking.

The following seven steps have been carefully designed to move you away from any present struggle and move you towards a place of rebalancing your emotional and physical life. By just "letting go of the oars" and floating upon the river for a short period of time, will automatically reset or return you back to that natural and default state - a calming place of ease, clear thought and tranquillity.

Although actively following these steps is certainly not mandatory, in my experience and the positive feedback from my students and clients, making these changes will bring both our bodies and our minds back into harmony and balance; to a place where we are at our best, without struggle and worry; for we can only do our best, at any one moment in time.

When planning a long journey, it is always advisable to take along certain items. Consider the following ideas and suggestions, as your luggage and prized possessions (for protection, for nutrition and vanity/luxury items) that you wish to take along for the ride.

The following steps should be carried out with the assistance and support of a medical professional. The speed and rate of success, finding a good mental/physical balance, will vary according to our own individual physical condition; mental stability; and general will-power.

Moreover, we should be less interested in the amount of time that we have to invest in doing something, especially when it is so beneficial to our overall health and well-being. We should consider not only the long-term physical benefits; but also, our personal quality of life; the lucidity of thought; and finally, keeping to any advancement or advancements made throughout the programme.

And, as we are only human, we have to accept that we are not always going to succeed in what we do; that setbacks are to be expected and natural; but the longevity and trend will indicate a positive way forward, which should keep us going when the going gets tough.

There are several applications or apps on the market, both free and payable, which have been suggested within this section. As most apps change over time, so please check for other similar apps after reading. **Please note: that the author advises caution when downloading and installing apps and is not responsible for any apps suggested within these pages.**

In the following part of this chapter, we will be examining those things that trigger or synchronise the internal and external influences of our natural body clocks. These triggers have been called Zeitgeber – from the German [tsateb] - literally "time giver". This was first used by the German physician, biologist and behavioural physiologist, Jürgen Aschoff and his team, who suggested that radically altering the day/night/sleep/wake cycles can, among other things, cause harmful consequences, such as a significant increase in mental illness. Aschoff's work indicated the existence of both internal (endogenous) "clocks" and external (exogenous) "cues" which synchronise both the biological rhythms and external influences of our bodies, which can, in turn, alter the timing of these internal clocks. The areas in which these Zeitgebers influenced his population were light, atmosphere, drugs, temperature, exercise and social interaction, together with the eating and drinking patterns of his subjects.

NB: all of these areas will be covered further on within this book.

In addition to this, having a good work/life balance, another significant area in our lives is the ability to rest, relax and sleep. So, having a good work/life/sleep (see graphic below) balance is key to living a long, healthy and positive life.

THE WORK/LIFE/SLEEP PYRAMID

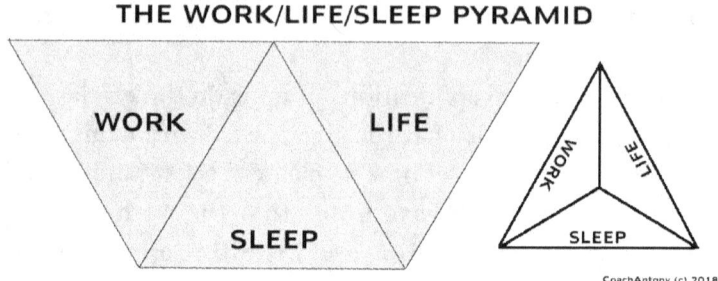

CoachAntony (c) 2018

As mentioned previously, the information in this book so far has been to offer the reader different options and suggestions regarding a whole host of themes and topics.

While reading the following **seven steps** and suggestions listed below, really consider if these ideas are for you. Judge if they feel "right" and not just theoretical or threatening, but really doable; and if they feel genuinely advantageous to your advancement and general well-being.

And, if you believe that some or all the suggestions below need to be taken on board or "worked upon"; or some crucial areas that you think you need to change or adjust in your life, then, by all means, start to slowly incorporate them into your daily routines; making them a habit, and decisively making them yours – however, importantly ... without stress or struggle!

1. Sleep

Sleep is nature's natural way of resting the mind (decreasing the ability to react to thoughts and stimuli) and at the same time allocating time to repair the body's vital systems, such as: helping to strengthen the immune system; replenishing our nervous system; repairing skeletal damage; and also, time to repair muscular abnormalities, this is called being in an *anabolic state*.

As mentioned previously, during sleep, the majority of our "key body systems" are in this anabolic state. In this phase, the body has the opportunity to regenerate, which in turn, helps to control our mood-swings during our waking hours; increases the long and short-term memory retention and recital; but also improves the performance of general cognitive thought throughout the day.

This is in contrast with the *catabolic state*, a phase which starts to breakdown large molecules into smaller units and gives the body the chemical energy necessary for the maintenance and the production of cells. Notable in this section is to remember that both the anabolism and catabolism states are mainly regulated and/or influenced by the circadian rhythm, the biological process within the body which repeats itself automatically over a period of about 24 hours.

While being in the process of sleeping, the body drifts between two different states of sleep: non-REM (NREM) and REM (Rapid Eye Movement). At the beginning of sleep, being in this NREM state, the body's temperature sinks; the heart rate or pulse slows, and the brain goes into a period of using less energy. In contrast, the REM phase (*also known as paradoxical sleep*) is much shorter than that of the NREM phase, and it is when dreaming is allowed, and the body restricts

61

the movement of muscle use, perhaps to avoid injury during sleep. These two sleep cycles repeat and follow each other - NREM/REM/NREM etc. Each phase lasts on average 90 minutes and occurs typically between 4 and 6 times within each normal sleeping session or cycle.

Regardless of our interest or belief in these facts regarding the sleep process, scientific research clearly shows that getting enough good quality sleep is crucial for the human body to thrive. And, the opposite is also true; that the lack of sleep causes all sorts of dysfunction, be that mental and physical illness within the body and mind; causing some forms of cancer and diabetes; encouraging depression; and increasing the likelihood of adipose or obesity. However, we should be able to know or feel an instinctive "rightness" or "wrongness" when considering our sleep patterns. When we are **not** getting enough sleep, we know that this is non-beneficial and having a direct effect on our general well-being.

There are many of useful apps on the market that will help us track and present our waking and sleeping moments, making them real and quantifiable. This data can then allow us to retrace and compare our moods swings, mental agility and sleepiness during the day, and contrast this with the amount of sleep we are getting. Having this data should then make it apparent that we need to regulate the number of hours of sleep so that we can allow the natural ability of our body to repair and heal itself. An example of one of these apps is called: **PrimeNap Sleep Tracker**. http://play.google.com/store/apps/details?id=com.primenap

With the introduction and development of artificial lighting, beginning with Edison's success with the electric light bulb, together with the first incandescent light in 1802 by Humphry

Davy, and later with the work of William Sawyer, Albon Man and Joseph Swan, these advancements or innovations have provided the world with a convenient and cheap artificial light source. Both for the home, but also in the workplace and especially at night, which has dramatically altered our natural sleeping patterns and consequently the length of our working day, at least in all first and second-world industrialised countries, plus an ever-increasing number of third-world countries, as well.

Our sleep patterns have also been exacerbated by new technological advancements in computing in general and more recently and more specifically with the availability, cheapness and connectivity of hand-held devices, such as tablets and smart-phones.

As mentioned previously, our innate and internal circadian rhythm or inner clock generally promotes sleep at night, however, with the beginning of the Fourth Industrial Revolution or 4IR, (encapsulating the advancement of artificial intelligence, driver-less vehicles, smart home appliances, 3D printing, etc.) light pollution in our big cities, plus the blueish light from our hand-held devices are causing significant problems with our ability to get a good night's sleep.

The Japanese word *Karoshi* is a term to describe death attributed to working to extremes. To combat this and the harsh working practices within the Japanese work-culture, many in Japan have adopted coping measures, such as sleeping while on duty or *Inemuri*. This is generally accepted there and has become somewhat the norm, especially with senior male managers, but less so accepted for the female employees in specific sectors.

Albeit, within the modern office, but especially with the introduction and standardisation of high LUX lighting or

LEDs, together with daylighting in office buildings, our human circadian rhythm and brains are being continually "tricked" by this synthetic, elongated day, leading to many researchers now arguing that this inhibits or alters our natural need for sleep.

People who have circadian rhythm sleep disorders and SAD (Seasonal Affective Disorder) are sometimes treated with light therapy (exposure to intense blueish white light during the day) to compensate for the lack of daylight in the winter months.

Consequently, in some larger more powerful companies, but especially in the banking and telecommunication sectors, the need for sleep has become increasingly stigmatised and even seen by some managers as a form of personal weakness and indicating, at the same time, disloyalty to the team, department and the overall company.

Sleep patterns have also dramatically changed over the years, owing perhaps to an increase in the option by the employer of working from home and consequently the non-necessity of being "present" in the workplace. There is still a lively ongoing debate between, on the other side, those that believe home office work is a form of empowerment for the employee; and on the other hand, companies and organisations increasingly expecting their employees to "subtly" work longer and extended hours, by being willing and available to deal with work problems at unsociable times, generally at the weekends or at night and certainly outside those regular working hours.

In the following section, we will be examining the use and misuse of alcohol. However, consuming alcoholic beverages can also affect sleep regularity and significantly change sleep patterns, which can, in turn, paradoxically cause a relapse from achieving sobriety by misuse and later may be a cause of insomnia, when alcohol is consciously and solely misused to achieve sleep and relaxation.

2. Alcohol, Caffeine, Medication and Drugs

Although recent research has shown, that consuming small quantities of alcoholic beverages in the evening, i.e. a small beer or a glass of wine, might actually reduce waking up in the middle of the night and/or increase the actual number of hours slept. However, for those who have trouble sleeping, these marked benefits change to disadvantages, when the dose is significantly increased or used over a more extended period.

Recreational drugs, including alcohol, the active ingredient of most beers, wines and distilled spirits, but also marijuana and hashish, nicotine in tobacco, caffeine in coffee and black tea, and other controlled substances and illegal drugs, e.g. methamphetamines, heroin, cocaine, LSD, Ecstasy, etc., force the body to do something unnatural and abnormal, deviating from having a potentially natural and well-being state.

Using and misusing mind-altering substances, such as those mentioned above, can be incredibly hard on the body in the long-term and weaning off these substances is also incredibly painful once the addiction has taken control and dependency and habit have been established.

Alcohol:

Alcohol, similar to caffeine products, is widely available and relatively cheap. Although alcoholic drinks have been consumed by humans since pre-historic times, the side effects and its addictive nature can cause significant damage to organs and even our DNA.

As with heavy smoking of tobacco, alcohol is classified as a Group One carcinogen by the International Agency for Research on Cancer (IARC), and, as so, heavy drinking increases the likelihood of developing certain cancers and liver disease.

Although, as mention previously, smaller and irregular doses of alcohol - a blood-alcohol concentration of 0.03%-0.12% - generally causes an improvement in mood, increases self-confidence and sociability. However, extreme misuse of alcohol - between 0.35% and 0.80% - may cause unconsciousness, respiratory problems, fatal alcohol poisoning and of lowering the life expectancy of humans by approximately ten years.

Recent studies have indicated that drinking small quantities of alcohol daily, e.g. one drink for women and two for men, is associated with a decreased risk of an early death, albeit an increase in heart disease, cirrhosis of the liver, plus damage to both the central and peripheral nervous systems, a loss of sexual desire and impotence in men and even diabetes.

Drinking alcohol, however, even in small quantities, generally slows the healing proficiency of the cells to repair damage to the DNA. Some research has even indicated that there is a positive relationship between dependency to alcohol and to having cravings, binge eating and general irritability in both men and women.

Caffeine:

Caffeine, readily available in the form of power drinks, coffee, tea, etc. can produce a mild form of drug dependency and addiction. The abrupt withdrawal of consumption can cause uncomfortable symptoms such as headaches, anxiety and general irritability for most people. There is, on average 80-175 mg of caffeine in a cup of coffee or energy drink. This caffeine, although mostly bitter to taste, generally mitigates tiredness, improves reaction times, aids wakefulness, improves concentration and coordination, for a short while after consumption. This "high" occurs typically after 60 minutes and dissipates after about four hours.

However, regular use or misuse of coffee and other products containing caffeine has a diverse number of side-effects. Caffeine may cause some to urinate more often and lose essential minerals. Moreover, a more significant long-term side effect is connected to the acidity from within the stomach (heartburn), which may also result in the consumer becoming overly anxious and can even cause long-term insomnia.

Medication:

There are on average 90 deaths a day in the US related to overdosing on opioids says the National Institute for Drug Abuse and having an economic burden of prescription opioid misuse is $78.5 billion a year. There are three types of medication, usually referred to when discussing non-medical medication misuse or self-medication of prescription drugs. These are Depressants: including barbiturates, benzo-diazepines and medication to assist in sleeping; Opioids: such as codeine, methadone and morphine are the most common; and Stimulants; amphetamines and methyl-phenidate.

The misuse of medication is generally considered as consuming a higher dosage than prescribed initially; taking the prescription drugs issued to another; using the medication in a different way other than recommended or intended and continuing on with the medication after the initial symptoms have subsided.

The reason for medication addiction, similar to alcohol addiction, are diverse and complex. The most significant and prevalent change over the decades has been the societal view and the acceptance of using medication to alleviate, mask or sugar-coat our negative emotions; emotions previously considered to be "normal" and part of life, for example: grief, sadness, loneliness, etc. instead of facing up to and dealing with the root of our problems.

The general ease and availability of prescribed medication has been encouraged by most doctors and physicians; promoted and given credence through advertising in the mass media; the deregulation and the increasingly unethical profit-driven pharmaceutical industry and, more significantly, from the sponsored lobbyists in government and research organisations.

Recreational Drugs:

It has been estimated that over 4 million people in the UK regularly use illicit drugs, with cannabis being the most common and widely available, followed by cocaine and ecstasy (MDMA) and lastly the newest available: K2, Spice, WAX, Flakka, etc. As with other mind-altering substances, street drugs, which are relatively easy to obtain, can become compulsive and or addictive; can have legal and psychological consequences, and is hard to control taking the correct dosage or amount with long-term use.

These might also cause several physical, mental, judicial, social problems and difficulties. Taking recreational drugs offers instant gratification but does not actually deal with the negative and emotional situations at hand; nor does it help to find a positive solution to a present problem.

3. Exercise, Movement and Sex

In our modern and hectic society, we have apparently lost the ability to move voluntarily and now, sadly equate exercise and movement with it being time-consuming, painful and generally causing discomfort.

As discussed later in this chapter, we have as a society gradually changed the traditional way we cook and feed ourselves. Moreover, fast food, technology and the internet have now removed that natural connection between buying, preparing, cooking and serving the food, rather than just ordering a nutritionless product online and having it delivered in a box a short time after.

Before, as hunters and gatherers, we had to expend a certain amount of energy to obtain enough food to live and survive. Now, however, with the emergence and availability of fast foods and fast food outlets, together with the dominance of frozen foods, processed foods and convenience foods becoming more prevalent since the 1960s, we now have developed an attitude of *extreme convenience*, which has turned us all into a society of laziness, chaotic calorie intake and an unhealthy lifestyle.

It is generally agreed that movement and exercise are incredibly important and necessary for staying healthy in the long-term. Doing any form of exercise releases those good-feeling hormones and BDNF (Brain-Derived Neurotrophic Factor) which heightens mood and the general feeling of well-being and happiness. We know intuitively that muscles need to be used; otherwise, they will lose their flexibility and efficiency. As mentioned before, to remain physically fit, healthy and active, now and in our older years, we need to do two types of exercise on a regular basis, aerobic and strength exercises.

Please always consult your doctor before beginning any new exercise regime. We are also generally over-estimating the amount of exercise that we are taking on a daily basis ... and using an app can check or correct this.

Aerobic:

Aerobic movement is using your limbs (arms and legs) to move your body which then significantly increases your heart-rate and breathing, while at the same time, strengthens physical endurance. This aerobic movement uses oxygen to burn fat and carbohydrates in your body, giving you the energy and, more importantly, a good healthy feeling. The most natural aerobic activity might be a brisk walk, a light jog, a short bike ride, or even taking the stairs instead of taking the elevator or lift. Moderate to intense aerobic exercise might be going on a long hike or trek in nature, swimming or undertaking a dance course. An intense and strenuous aerobic exercise might involve an active and fast-moving sport, such as tennis, squash, basketball, etc.

Aerobic exercise can also be beneficial when losing weight, when combined with a suitable calorie controlled diet, but exercise, in general, can also reduce the chances of dementia or Alzheimer's Disease later on in life, by reducing the build-up of Beta-Amyloid (a sticky, toxic protein) in the brain, which is shown to affect the connectivity within the brain and eventually kills the brain cells. This type of exercise can also reduce the chances of getting high blood pressure and diabetes; together with reducing the probability of having strokes, as well as getting some forms of cancer and even heart disease, later in life.

Anaerobic:

Anaerobic exercise uses only certain types of muscles and burns mostly the carbohydrates in the food that we eat. Activities such as lifting weights or doing sit or push-ups are essential because they increase muscle formation, they also assist in building those muscle groups which support the spine and bones, and lastly, anaerobic training increases your body's strength and overall endurance.

Both anaerobic and aerobic exercise used interchangeably, are essential for maintaining a healthy body and therefore, promoting a healthy lifestyle. As mentioned previously, aerobic movement can make your heart muscle stronger, but it can also increase the number of red blood cells throughout the body, which in turn, increases the amount of oxygen in your bloodstream, and thus gives the body that extra bit of power and energy during the day.

Anaerobic movement and exercise not only strengthen the bones in our bodies but also reduces the chances of developing osteoporosis. This type of daily activity also protects the tendons, ligaments and even the functions of joints; it can reduce muscle pain and muscle injury later in life; it can also improve overall cardiac strength; and, finally, it can even increase the levels of good cholesterol in the body.

Ask any professional runner, those athletes that run the 26 miles of a marathon, and they will explain that it takes an enormous amount of time, training and preparation long before running the actual race. So being realistic about your current fitness levels, perhaps being overweight, unfit or just out of practice, and not putting ourselves under an enormous amount of pressure at the beginning, is paramount.

Our goal here is to be realistic. We must start off by just being generally more active daily. Walking at a brisk pace, approximately 12,000 steps a day, or going for a bike ride for at least one to one and a half hours is a great first step. By doing this, you are getting out and moving, taking in more oxygen and, at the same time, using your major muscles.

Especially at the beginning, if you are feeling unfit, you know intuitively that you do not want to overdo things and moderation is always the best rule of thumb. However, we need to spend less time sitting and being inactive and more time moving. We need to move so that our breathing and heart rate increases, and our bodies can gradually adjust to this new active and healthy way of life.

When talking about doing regular muscle-strengthening exercises, we also should remember that we will either use our muscles or we will lose them. Building and sustaining muscle growth is vival for general well-being and movement, together with keeping our bones strong; regulating our blood-pressure and our blood-sugar levels and keeping our weight down and within a healthy level, are all things that we need to control and keep in mind when thinking holistically about our general health and well-being. Controlling and cutting back on your intake of sugar - both indirect and direct forms and also getting Type 2 diabetes - decreases the risk of developing dementia later in life.

As mentioned before, exercise does not only strengthen the heart muscle but also improves memory, i.e. remembering, storing and retrieving information, by increasing the size of the hippocampus, which is essential for memory in the brain. To sum up, any type of exercise or movement increases the BDNF (Brain-derived neurotrophic factor) protein or chemical which encourages the growth of nerve connections and helps in the formation of new brain cells.

Sex:

Most people have both the desire to belong to "something" more significant than themselves and also to feel part of a broader social group. We all have the need or necessity to interact with others and to feel "part of" something bigger than just ourselves.

Similarly, love is generally searched for from other people who we find sexually and emotionally attractive, but also biologically, by those who we subtly consider would make the best off-spring (combining the two DNA codes). However, when this "wanting" of an intimate partner or close relationship

72

gets negatively affected by stress, illness, life circumstances, etc., then these "needs and wants" require some form of compensatory action, resulting sometimes in some sort of addictive or socially deviant behaviour; addiction to sex; sex with strangers; sex in unusual places; Swinging; and the use of prostitutes, etc.

Sexual addiction, hypersexual disorder and those with sexual dependency issues are people who are unable to control their physical urges related to sexual desires and behaviours.

These excessive sexual desires, Satyriasis for men and Nymphomania for women, are not generally considered to be addictions, in the usual sense, but rather seen as a compulsive behaviour or having an impulse control disorder. Similar to those who have the symptoms of a Borderline Personality Disorder, those that experience these excessive sexual desires, typically having had a long history of abnormal behaviour, such as having had many unstable relationships, having mixed and rapid emotions; a negative sense of self; also have a general lack of trust in other people as well.

4. Spending and Gambling
Spending/Shopping:
Compulsive Buying Disorder, Oniomania and being a shopaholic are all characterised by an extreme impulse or obsession with shopping for things and the need to buy things in general. It is much easier today with the convenience of having the opportunity to shop when the stores are closed. Internet shopping, shopping channels and teleshopping on television offer a direct connection to buying things and having them delivered soon after that. However, there are many adverse consequences of *needing* to do this activity. This uncontrollable urge, for some, is not only time-consuming but can also lead to

real financial problems and social difficulties. Customarily associated with other disorders, like having high anxiety, bulimia and substance abuse, oniomania affects many with those who have a low ability to cope with stress and mood swings, but most believe that it is rooted in perfectionism from childhood and a deep-seated searching for validation through the shopping experience.

After a shopping spree, many experience buyer's remorse, shown through guilt and a realisation of the relapse. After that to combat this feeling, they need to shop some more to alleviate that feeling. The consequences and stigma involved plays a big part in the aftermath of a shopping spree. Together with the probability of accumulating too much stuff at home and the debt involved. To hide the embarrassing compulsion, the newly bought goods are often destroyed or hidden.

Gambling:

Similar to extreme shopping, those who gamble regularly, playing the odds against the *house*, believe that staking money on an uncertain outcome, in the hope of winning it big, is an easy and quick way to achieve success and significance. They believe that this "short-cut" will not only make themselves feel better about themselves in the short-term but will also show their own "success" to others, probably lacking in other areas of their lives.

The idea of betting money for enjoyment can quickly become addictive and harmful to the vast majority of people. This addiction, as part of the obsessive-compulsive disorder, can be caused by an insufficient amount of the hormone serotonin. Although there has been a certain amount of success in helping those with a gambling addiction, like those with acute depression (using a higher dosage of antidepressants), not dealing with the real and underlying mental thought patterns, limits the usefulness and success of the medication in the long-term.

Research has indicated that the reason why we gamble, generally stems from an acute feeling of disempowerment within the home, at work or even in the wider society. They are always "hoping" to change those underlying and constant feelings of disempowerment and disenchantment of their perceived healthy lives and striving to achieve "the chance to win" just one more time; to take-back control of their lives; and to finally prove that they are indeed worthy, useful and successful.

The *house*, i.e. casinos, scratch cards, the lottery, betting shops, one-armed bandits, etc., by the nature of the business concept, will always win in the long-term. So the striving to take back control and gaining power once again of one's life, by using a corrupt but legal system, having the "odds stacked against you", will inevitably lead to a continuation of these negative feelings of frustration and depression, but also paradoxically, will continue the dependency on gambling, trying in vain to rectify the perceived problem or an unjust situation.

5. **Water and Hydration**

Following oxygen, water is the most important, yet often taken for granted, substance needed to provide the body with what it needs to survive and makes up more than half of the body's weight. Sufficient consumption of water assists in removing waste from our bodies; keeps the body both warm and cool when necessary; assists in the movement of joints; and finally provides the main building blocks for blood production. Although the amount and types of liquids we should consume daily has been under scrutiny and discussed over the past few decades, it is still very affordable, readily available, generally free of contaminants and safe to drink from the tap in most industrial and post-industrial countries.

Although the quality of tap water has significantlyimproved over the years, other man-made pollutants are now being realised in the environment, such as: microplastic particle pollution in our waterways and oceans (and consequently in the fish being caught). Similarly, ground and drinking water, are both being contaminated by synthetic hormones, for example: ethinyl estradiol originating from contraceptive pills; together with toxic and bioaccumulative water pollutants and poisons, such as arsenic, lead, mercury, and cadmium; plus the leaching, run-off, fertigation and seepage of animal manure, pesticides, fertilisers (nitrogen and phosphorus), fungicides, insecticides and herbicides from fields into the nearby rivers and groundwater caused by modern mega-agricultural farming methods and the pharmaceutical and chemical industries. Some argue that big business and the manufacturers of these products should be held responsible for their role in causing the release of these pollutants and be asked or forced into investing in the purification and filtration of the water. At present, instead of cleaning the origins of drinking water, lakes, rivers and reservoirs, the consumer is having to deal with these problems at the "end of pipe treatments", using, e.g. portable water filtration systems after the water leaves the tap or faucet.

The guidelines recommend that on average an adult requires about 2 - 2,5 litres - (70 imp fl oz; 68 US fl oz) per day for adult women and (88 imp fl oz; 85 US fl oz per day for adult men) - of water a day to remain healthy, this includes the total amount of liquids consumed, pure drinking water and beverages, plus the natural water found in the foods that we eat.

When we are feeling thirsty, this typically means that the

body is already lacking water and is in a dehydrated state. The colour of your urine, usually colourless or light yellow/green, indicating that you are well hydrated; and dark green or brown you are most likely dehydrated; is also a good indicator, together with having symptoms of dehydration, such as having headaches, dryness of the mouth and darkness around the lower parts of the eyes. When we are talking about (de)hydration of the body, we usually think about drinking pure water and not the beverages we consume, such as coffee, tea, beer, wines and the trending sport and energy drinks now available.

However, these beverages all contribute to satiating our thirst and providing the body with the necessary liquids needed. Consider that some sports drinks, although providing water, carbohydrates and electrolytes to the body, can also contain excessive amounts of sugar and salt. Energy drinks also contain large amounts of caffeine, ginseng, guarana and taurine. These are things that our bodies generally do not require and act to overstimulate the brain. Surprisingly, with this in mind, recent indications are showing that in the US there is now a marked increase in the consumption of bottled sparkling and still water, overtaking that of fizzy sugary drinks or sodas.

A natural alternative to these drinks might be eating more fruit and vegetables, such as watermelon, tomatoes and cucumbers, as a way of increasing the daily amount of water, but more healthily. Despite the cost and inconvenience of carrying water to your home, together with the media's general reporting of the quality of water in your area, more than likely, it is the taste that dictates the choice to pay for expensive bottled water. However, the flat taste and the chlorine smell of tap water, especially in large towns and cities, may be an essential and determining factor as well - also important is plastic pollution.

6. **Food, nutrition, weight and stamina**

As the topic of food and nutrition is vast, diverse and complicated, we are just going to concentrate on the two main but important trends: organic food, in general; and snacking, in particular; both have influenced the way we now eat in the modern world.

Food:

"Let food be your medicine and medicine your food" was a maxim from Hippocrates around 400 BC. Two thousand years later, it was William Prout who researched and came up with the hypothesis that foods can be divided up into three major types: carbohydrates, fats and proteins, all of which serve our bodies.

As an organism, we need to eat to remain healthy and get energy from our food. This was determined in the past by the availability of different foodstuffs dependant on the season. This has now changed through modern harvesting and new cultivation techniques.

However, these existential, basic needs are still present, but now just dormant in the back of our minds. It takes real willpower, concentrated knowledge and action to reduce these cravings, at least in the beginning, for things to eat, which will benefit us and our bodies.

Since the 1980s there has been a significant decline in cooking the food we consume within the home, owing to the prevalence of fast food chains, the advances in processed foods and the indoctrination of making snacking (eating sugary snacks between meals) more acceptable and normal.

Although the idea of snacking has been around in the US since the 1950s, it only truly arrived in the UK in the 1970s, offering, mainly children, *"a treat"* between meals.

Organic food production, on the other hand, concentrates

on renewable resources, the conservation of soil and water to produce and improve the general quality of the environment and has been growing in popularity since the 1970s. It has, up until recently, been a more expensive alternative for its dedicated followers, customers and consumers.

However, despite the laws and regulations governing the production of organic food, the organic and free-range farmers strive to promote an ecological balance of the foodstuffs which they grow and bring to the marketplace. There is also an ever-increasing emphasis on the promotion of being ecological in balance with the land and sea (its carbon footprint impact), but also sees variety and variability of life on earth through biodiversity, and more significantly, restricting the amount and types of certain pesticides and fertilisers. Later in the process, they also look at food additives used in farming, the packaging and correct labelling of products and have major animal-welfare concerns.

Since then, and after a significant increase in both farmers markets and health food shops beginning to dominate the market, the big retailers decided to offer a similar organic alternative, for a price similar or the same as their smaller retailers; generally, probably not because they believe in the sustainability and better taste of the product, but because they were rapidly losing market share. On a similar note, there has also been a growing number of people opting to refrain from eating animal products and those vegans who believe that they do not wish to encroach on the animals and insects in any way at all.

This trend has been mainly due to an increase in the mega-mergers of large companies and corporations within the food and beverage industries. These giant corporations, especially in China, the new agricultural powerhouse, together with the major supermarket chains, mega stores and discounters, work together and now control the lion's share of the market. They also dictate, not only the brands and produce that we find on our supermarket shelves, but also the prices, sizes and quantities of these goods.

Smaller independent retailers from the past, i.e. the family-run butcher, local baker, experienced fishmonger and high street grocer, etc., despite being closer to home, friendlier and certainly more convenient, have, over the years, largely been wiped out by the dominance of the larger supermarket chains. These larger chains have forced their smaller competitors out of the market, mostly by using anti-competitive predatory pricing policies and offering special offers, such as BOGOF (Buy One Get One Free) to lure the traditional customers into their shops and away from the smaller high street stores.

The philosophy and marketing strategy behind the large food manufacturers of today is to make a product which is both convenient and cheaper in price, rather than if you bought the various ingredients separately and cooked the same meal at home.

These giant concerns and conglomerates can produce in a short period, and in vast quantities, a single product using industrial-scale basic ingredients, something that is unattainable by a person cooking at home or even a chef in a small restaurant. Similarly, purchasing and using bulk industrial-strength ingredients, in large-scale production can significantly lower the price on the supermarket shelves, which then increases the profit margin and availability. All this without the consumer fully knowing that this cheaper product has probably been made using not only inferior core ingredients, such asthe adulteration of honey with rice syrup to supply the demand but also having the quality and goodness (micronutrients, minerals, trace elements, vitamins, fibre, etc.) removed.

Also, depending where you are in the world, there has been an increase in "dual-quality foods and products". These are brand products being sold in some second and third world countries, using cheaper alternatives and sub-standard ingredients in the manufacturing process. They contain different levels and types of fats (trans fats), oils (palm oil) and using fructose and glucose syrup instead of sugar, as well as synthetically made sweeteners such as aspartame and acesulfame.

Nutrition:

We have, as consumers, lost the natural connection between the cellophane packages on the supermarket shelves and the natural and original origins of our food.

We have not only lost the ability to cook and prepare our own food, something learned and passed down to the younger generation by a parent, grandparent or elder guardian, but also the knowledge of buying separate products needed for that meal, together with understanding the nutritional value of each item and the process and expertise of cooking the ingredients to produce and serve a tasty and appetising meal.

Whereas before, it was the woman or housewife that stayed at home and prepared the meals for the rest of the family, now, in the post-industrial and modern society, with gender role changes and financial necessity, it is still generally the woman who prepares and cooks the meals for the family. However, she now must do this *"on top"* of doing her job or career outside the home. It is not surprising that there has been an increase in convenience foods, making preparing and eating food at home quicker and less complicated.

Modern apartments and houses generally now either have a small, make-shift kitchen area, containing only a microwave, fridge and sink or conversely have a brand new, modern kitchen which is hardly ever used.

In the US, as well as in the UK, there have been many strategies over the years to try to positively change how each population eats. The MyPlate idea suggested that we should divvy-up our meals having 30% whole grains, 40% vegetables, 10% fruits and only 20% different types of proteins, plus an extra plate for dairy products such as a glass of 1% fat milk or natural, unsweetened yoghurt.

There is reliable advice given in these programmes about reducing the daily amount of food eaten, but also limiting or cutting back on added salt and sugars. Essential minerals and fatty acids, such as Omega-3, 6 and 9, are extremely important for the body to remain healthy and these should be added, with the following foodstuffs, to your diet if possible:

Omega-3: Mackerel, Salmon, Cod liver oil, walnuts, chia seeds, Herring, flaxseeds (grounded), Tuna, Whitefish, Sardines, hemp seeds, Anchovies, Brussels sprouts, kale, spinach and watercress and egg yolks.

Omega-6: Sunflower seeds, walnuts, sesame seeds, pine nuts, Brazil nuts, pecan nuts, pumpkin seeds, peanuts, almonds, butter, eggs, parmesan, whole milk, ham and bacon, lamb, whole grain bread, etc.

And **Omega-9**, this can be produced by our bodies, but can also be found in olive oil, avocados, almonds, sunflower oil, pistachios, cashews, hazelnuts, macadamia nuts, etc. and can reduce the risk of heart disease and strokes by freeing blocked arteries, etc.

Owing to the advancement of modern food production, and

the increase of processed foods, in particular, these necessary micro-nutritional ingredients are missing in most of the fast food meals that we now eat.

Sugar, both granular and what is naturally found in food, and salt have been consumed in ever-increasing amounts over the last 50 years, so that our taste buds now expect extremely salty and sugary flavours in the foods that we buy and eat. The addictive nature of sugar, increasing the pleasure senses of our brain, has been causal in promoting addictions, and, consequently has also been linked to causing certain diseases and afflictions, such as obesity and diabetes, as well as heart disease.

Big business, shareholders and executives have all been criticised for being less interested in the general health of the people that they sell their products to, but rather the profits made for the company and its shareholders. These big businesses have become major players in the modern economy, offering products with an ever-increasing shelf life and lower price tags, which have all greatly influenced the political agenda, regarding agricultural spending and nutritional trends, as seen in the introduction of snacking and providing fast foods for children in schools:

See Jamie Oliver (School Dinners). https://en.m.wikipedia.org/wiki/Jamie%27s_School_Dinners

Weight and Stamina:

In most western industrialised countries, there has been a significant increase in the levels of obesity and being overweight of the adult population. In the UK there is only a slight gender difference between the percentage of men 65% to that of women 58%.

The amount of food that adult needs to function adequately

is generally dependent on age, gender, build and how physically fit he or she is. The best advice is to get the help of a doctor or trained nutritionist to assist in finding an ideal daily intake of calories. In general, men usually need around 2,500 calories (10,500kJ) and women about 2,000 calories (8,400kJ) to remain both fit and healthy. If overweight or obese, then this figure should be significantly reduced over a long period, thus making the dieting process less painful and having a higher chance of success in the long run.

As mention previously, finding and putting in place the right diet is essential to living a long, active and healthy life. However, the extra added sugar and salt in many modern-day foods has masked the calorie intake receptors of the brain, meaning that we are now eating and drinking far more than our bodies actually want or need and are storing this "surplus" in body fat.

This fat is not only what is shown externally, but also hidden within and surrounding the core organs, such as the heart, liver, kidneys, etc. This extra surplus fat that we are then carrying around with us has a multitude of negative impacts upon our day to day living, including general lethargy, dullness in thinking, slowness of movement and making the body more susceptible to Type 2 diabetes, strokes, heart disease and even some cancers.

We should also look at why we eat when sometimes we are just bored or depressed instead of being truly hungry. One of the many hunger hormones released into the blood is called Ghrelin (Growth, Hormone, Release Inducing) or lenomorelin and is released into the blood when the stomach is empty and moves towards the brain - which ultimately tells us that we are hungry, but at the same time also controls the amount of energy used and is needed. However, this trigger can be easily blocked by stress and other significant traumatic events.

With the help of modern technology, it has now become more manageable in controlling and reducing the number of calories daily. There are many different types of calorie counter apps in the app stores, most are free, easy to use and can help with understanding where those extra calories are coming from; an example of one of these apps is called: MyFitnessPal: https://play.google.com/store/apps/details?id=com.myfitnesspal.android

It should be a realistic aim to lose half a kilo each week until you have reached, or hovering around, your target weight and waist size. It is essential and necessary to celebrate each half kilo dropped and to check and chart the progress made daily.

To find your ideal weight - evaluating your age, height and gender - use one of the many BMI (Body Mass Index) calculators or apps online. https://play.google.com/store/apps/details?id=com.smart.bmi.calculator.healthy.weight.loss

However, using such BMI calculators without expert advice might lead to unrealistic and false readings. This is because the BMI model alone cannot take into account if the person has more muscle or fat; if that person is slender or big built; or leads an active/lethargic lifestyle.

Being mindful about your eating habits, enjoying and eating proper, healthy food at regular intervals, will undoubtedly help to reduce cravings and the number of times we eat between meals, especially when we are under stress, sad or bored (comfort eating). Similarly, snacking in the evening on crisps, chocolate and sugary drinks, which contain a lot of sugars and are high in fats, while mindlessly watching television or surfing the web, can also add to an invisible load of extra calories and is certainly **not** conducive to mindful eating.

Believing in the labelling and marketing of a product; just because something is labelled as *"healthy"* or *"wellness"* or *"low in fat"*, does not necessarily mean that it is healthy and good for you. Spend more time reading the labels and find out how much sugar a "low fat" product has. Let us not also forget that most alcoholic beverages also contain a lot of calories; scan the code of the bottle or tin using the app, to get more information about the product.

Before eating a meal, drink a glass of water and, more importantly, when you feel *nearly* full … stop eating and wait twenty minutes or so. The satiation of the food from the stomach will take a while for this "full-up feeling" to reach and tell the brain that you are in fact full and satisfied. We eat with our eyes too, for this reason, consider getting smaller plates to trick the mind in believing that there is a lot of food on the plate.

Become more knowledgeable with the different foodstuffs and their calories. After a time, you will know instinctively just what will make up your daily calorie allowance.

It is also essential to take a relaxed, bird's-eye view of this new way of eating and drinking and do not be too hard on yourself if you binge or eat more calories that are on your daily allowance. Find foods that you enjoy for different times of the day. For example, for breakfast eat porridge or muesli with no sugar just fruit and perhaps ginger, this is a excellent source of fibre and is filling and comforting. Also, eating some sort of dietary fibre in the morning will help to absorb excess water from the body and helps to remove waste from the intestines. For lunch or dinner, choose a meal with whole grains or whole foods, brown rice, or a mixed salad, etc., and avoid nutrient-poor processed foods if possible. As our bodies digest these whole grains and whole foods more slowly, these foods can keep us satisfied much longer, which can stop cravings, snacking, and us eating more than necessary. However, changing diet and eating more whole grains and fresh produce can be difficult, especially in the beginning.

Eating dark chocolate (containing more than 70% cocoa), which contains potassium, zinc, selenium and iron, plus having anti-inflammatory qualities and a convenient source of antioxidants, instead of eating other types of low cocoa chocolate bars on the market, is ideal for extinguishing those cravings for sweet things after a meal and late at night.

These cravings, when the brain indicates that you are hungry and essentially going to die if you can not find food, can sometimes be alleviated by drinking a glass of water - it might just be that you are only dehydrated, rather than hungry.

The act of daily meditation can also help to realise or notice things more mindfully, by, for example, being tempted with something sweet or unhealthy, especially if you are on a calorie controlled diet. By meditating regularly (see Chapter Nine) we tend to use the executive functions of our brain more, which helps us to make healthy decisions about what we eat and assists in avoiding those sugary things, especially when there are healthy alternatives available.

However, we sometimes still use or misuse alcohol and food as a way of changing our emotions and the way we are feeling in the moment, without actually dealing with the underlying cause of the discomfort or thought. Notice and become aware of these urges, and correct this compulsion immediately, if possible, by doing something positive instead, i.e. sport, meditation, walking, reading, talking, etc.

As mentioned previously, fruit and vegetables are a great source of vitamins, minerals and fibre and should make up about a third of the total amount of food we eat daily. If you cannot afford to eat fresh fruit or vegetables you can use frozen, tinned or dried alternatives, although this might be less nutritious and containing more sugars, but still better than not eating these types of foods at all.

7. **Technology and Other People**

It has never been easier to connect and stay connected to family, friends, colleagues and the workplace, via the technological advancement of hand-held devices and the connectivity/availability of having a fast internet connection in most places. We are social beings, and the idea of sharing ideas, thoughts, fears, concerns and experiences is something that our social selves enjoy, protect and strive for. SMS, e-mail and instant messaging, such as Messenger, Whatsapp, FaceTime, Skype, etc., has made staying in contact with these people and groups much more accessible, more immediate and certainly more convenient.

However, although these technological innovations have significantly reduced the number of hours of direct face-to-face communication at work, some companies are now suggesting to their employees, at all hierarchical levels, to reinstate this once informal and direct form of communication between colleagues and even the clients.

We have become afflicted or held hostage to the ever increasing "instantness" of the moment. To search for and research things instantaneously about what is happening in the world, together with being at the *beck and call* of an ever-increasing, unrealistic expectation of being *willing and able* to reply to a message or request 24 hours a day, seven days a week.

This perceived mandatory **social media attentiveness** of

being online and available 24 hours a day, being connected to the hive, controlled and monitored by the subtle use of cookies and GPS positioning of handheld devices, raises compelling health questions and convincing privacy issues.

Social media, as an innovation from the powerful internet, together with computer gaming and television, are probably the worse and best time wasters of the modern era. Before we know it, the day has come to an end, and we have to consider, what exactly have we got to show for this expended and ultimately limited time?

It is certainly recommended that taking time away from social media for a few hours, days or months is highly recommended at regular intervals. Even better might be switching your phone to "flight mode" when you are not actively using or looking for something specific and switching off the notification sounds which interrupt our "*now*" time. The weekends and during our holidays should be a time to unwind, relax and reduce the stress from those regular days; and not a time to recover from the worry and pressure of the week or weeks beforehand. For those people who find it hard to "switch off" there are now hotels and resorts which cater for those guests by offering a purposely internet free accommodation - a relaxing black hole environment - to do other things.

You will find a lot more time in your life to do other things; and even if you do not, you will experience boredom (something expected and normal to most people in days gone by.) We are all guilty of the fear of missing out (FOMO) by switching off our mobile devices, for even a minute or two.

Recent research has found extra sensors in the eye, called the Intrinsically Photosensitive Retinal Ganglion cells, which picks up light at night, mainly the blue/white light of computer monitors, smartphones or tablets, and tricks our brain to believe that it is time to stay awake, when it should be telling us that it is time to sleep.

By being aware of the time, you spend using your electronic devices will help you see and understand your patterns of daily use. Using an app, such as "App Usage" you can track your everyday use, which might rob you from precious hours from the day, and using this extra time to "escape" from the buzz of the hive, allows more actual time to be used for creative thought and relaxation. Relishing this "being in the nothingness of time" enable effective plans to be drawn up and is different from being or feeling lonely.

Being *"solitudual"* just means … allowing yourself to have a moment. Like catching up with an old friend, this taking a moment just slows things down and, at the same time, connects you to that inner voice, rather than being continually connected to the information overload of the hive, giving you a pure, quiet clarity - a rare commodity at any time.

When the mind is put on pause, it allows the brain to access memories, thoughts and emotions from the past, which might just offer a solution to problem-solving in the present.

By reading posts, interesting articles from the internet or in an old-fashioned newspaper, this can reverse the build-up of the Beta-Amyloid and, at the same time, increase our Cognitive Reserve - a term referring to using other parts of the brain, to perform specific tasks - and reading can also decrease general cognitive impairment of brain function.

Other People:

This cognitive reserve, mentioned previously, can also be stimulated by doing or learning something new, but also when socialising. You are looking to get a support system into place, in order to assist you – if and when needed. Before entering into battle, it is always wise to seek out who is on your side (allies) and those who might be against you (foes).

Many of us have been brought up or raised not to accept help from others, no matter how hard things got in our lives. Simply put, we are now most likely going to need help, perhaps from a partner, a good friend or colleague, a doctor, coach or psychologist, or someone you can genuinely trust.

This feeling of being obligated or of being indebted to a third-party, most likely is a learned response and stems from a previous time, albeit an unhelpful time, that has little or no relevance to this modern era. With our communicative and technologically adjoined lifestyles; being that most of us are now totally connected and interdependent of others through advanced technology, or through screen-time, there is now a constant and perpetual need or addiction for interconnected-ness.

8

MANY PATHS

"Many roads lead to the path, but basically there are only two: reason and practice."
Bodhidharma

If you absolutely knew, without a shadow of a doubt, that your future plans and life would be relatively safe, would this knowledge and connected emotion alleviate any or all of the fears of making a mistake or taking the next step or decision?

Similarly, if you were sure that your next planned journey, perhaps without signposts or advice from others, would turn out *well*, and that you would eventually arrive at the most fantastic destination, but most likely different from what you first expected or planned, would this change your future decision-making strategy?

We are generally not fearful of that which we know. Yes, employers are certainly going to change things in the working environment in the future which will, directly and indirectly, affect its workforce; this is normal and improvements to the services and systems should be expected, anticipated and perhaps even welcomed.

However, in the eyes of your boss or manager, what might be less expected is that you, as an employee, should now be more prepared to firstly, notice these changes and, perhaps more importantly, hopefully, be able to *deal* with them more neutrally, because of your newly acquired way of thinking. You should now know more about what you want and be less fearful and more prepared for the path which is unfolding beneath your feet.

Below are suggestions and reminders for getting our minds and bodies in the best possible place to be, and puts the points offered from the previous chapter into a practical and less theoretical setting.

Your Body:

Consider if it is actually true, that you do not have enough time to look after your body? Just get out more and go for a short walk; feel the rightness of walking; experience the lack of stress or hurrying; take time to observe the environment around you. This is all about being in the moment and being in the movement of your body.

Together with getting out more, we can also use our technology to help us. Every other day do some sort of weight-training exercise, this 15 minute workout on YouTube is excellent, needing only some weights, preferably dumbbells: HASFIT 15 Minute Beginner Weight Training https://youtu.be/U0bhE67HuDY

YouTube is an excellent resource for changing your body and weight. Once you feel comfortable doing the 15-minute workout, you can then move on to something a little more strenuous and advanced: 30 Min Beginner Weight Training for Beginners Workout Strength Training Dumbbell Workouts Women Men - https://youtu.be/jDF4XiUtXGM.

The day after running or doing weight-training, you might notice your muscles feeling tight or stiff. This is normal and should be expected! You are using muscles that you do not usually use, which at the same time shows your progress, but also your lack of fitness in this area. Despite this, it is essential not to stop. Many people give up on that day, but that is precisely the time, **not** to give up! *Important:* Working through these 15 minutes to exercise every day will eventually get easier, and you will feel better about yourself, too, knowing that you are doing something special and unique for yourself.

Your Body Weight:

Ideally, we should find a happy body-weight for ourselves. An inner knowing regarding what is a comfortable and realistic weight to aim for and to try and sustain. You can do this with the help of a personal trainer or doctor, but this ideal weight should be intuitive and visceral, we should feel comfortable in our own bodies. Also ask other people who know you for their opinions, so that you have something different than your own subjective view of self.

What your body needs:

Although there is sometimes a reason for taking nutritional supplements and medication for some illnesses, mainly depression and perhaps OCD, your body generally knows "intuitively" what it *wants*, what it *needs* and will indicate this *by craving* this or that. For example, a Vitamin C deficiency will lead to a craving for oranges. However, as sugar is now specifically and purposely added to most processed foods, this has over the years "*masked*" these natural cravings, and as sugar is, by nature, addictive, it is going to be harder to correctly "listen" to what is needed, rather than to that long-term subliminal addiction.

To have a fully functioning body, we first need to be fully aware of what our bodies need daily and then establish a doable and workable plan to provide this for the long-term. Start out slowly, begin by gradually eating something healthy with each of your regular meals and slowly add more and more ingredients recommended from this book (see recipes at the end of this book). After a few weeks, this will become almost routine and will positively affect your thought processes and significantly increase your long-term memory.

Eating Better:

Cutting back on sugary snacks between meals and replacing them with fruit or water is a great and easy place to start. There are a few recipes in the back of this book to offer tasty doable recipes, especially if you are presently struggling with money or cooking for a large family. Definitely consider cooking your own food whenever possible, strive to eat smaller portions each day and at the same time buying smaller plates to eat from. This will make the portions and meals look and seem more significant than they actually are. Eat only when you are hungry. Eat slowly and consciously enjoy the food you are eating. Find that place "*before*" you feel fully satisfied or full. Remember that the sugar that you have been eating has "*blurred*" this stopping mechanism in the body, plus it takes a certain amount of time (about 20 minutes) for the fullness of the stomach to reach the brain.

Water:

In the beginning, you might need to schedule your water consumption, rather than when you feel like it or feel thirsty.

There needs to be a routine set, and by using your smartphone calendar to notify you every hour or so is highly advisable. Remember, too, that drinking enough water daily is very helpful in losing weight and undoubtedly crucial for the body and brain to function well.

Keeping Mentally Active:

Consider keeping your mind active with a variety of different training programmes or courses. Remember that within most companies, the yearly training budget is never wholly used. However, please ensure, if your company is offering training to its employees, that there is, in fact, enough time to take time out during the day to complete this and **never** be prepared to do these training courses in your own time, i.e. at home or in the evenings.

Undertaking a training programme during the day is always beneficial, similar to taking a lunch break or having a coffee with colleagues. It offers the employee a time-out from the hectic pace of modern business and a timely respite, plus the chance to reboot and do something different during the working day.

Alcohol-free beverages:

Although having an occasional alcoholic drink, our alcohol consumption, in general, should also be kept in check. Although alternative beverages, without alcohol, are now more readily available, and most even contain fewer calories than the same beverages with alcohol, we should still be aware of using or misusing alcohol in times of stress and/or insomnia.

At work mapping:

Similar to mapping out our sleep patterns regularly, it might also be advantageous to map-out when we work and how we work. Consider when we are the most efficient during the day and try to keep the number of hours "at work" regular and stable.

In Japan, some larger companies have now found that turning off the office lighting at 7pm prevents its employees from working late into the night and not having enough time to fully recover, after a long day in the office. Working late or coming in early has been encouraged in some countries with perks, such as offering an early communal breakfast or dinner when one works late. People in Europe still find it curious that, despite having significantly less day's holiday, some employees in the US do not use **all** their yearly paid holidays.

Our days off should be a time to really switch off and do other things, with family, friends and a time to follow our hobbies, rather than helping the company be even more profitable and successful, perhaps at the cost of our health and general well-being. In some Scandinavian countries it is part of the dominant working culture to take part in the daily "fika"; to leave the desk, drink coffee, eat something sweet and chat with other colleagues. An excellent way to switch off and get a new perspective about what we are doing and, more importantly, have more personal contact with other colleagues at the same time.

The things we take for granted:

We take so many things for granted in our lives. Even the fact that we are alive is a miracle and incredible in its own right. We, more than likely, live in a society where many things are just expected; i.e. healthcare, electricity, clean drinking water, infrastructure, technology, a secure place to sleep, friends, family, a loving partner, etc. The fact that the sun comes up each morning; or the night skies, full of stars; and the fact that we are here to observe these events ... is a gift and should never, ever be taken for granted. When we pay taxes to our government or society, this money is used, among other things, for institutions and the infrastructure; i.e. libraries, schools, roads, etc. We also pay taxes to our government so that they can protect and represent us.

Passing on Knowledge:

Joseph Campbell explores the notion of the Hero's Journey, a journey bound in myth, but nevertheless passed on through the generations. Most of these passed down necessary skills, and general knowledge have been lost, forgotten or ignored over the recent decades, owing to major advances in technology, access to healthcare, convenience foods, etc.

However, these necessary skills and necessities, i.e. how to cook a meal from scratch; knowing the different edible plants in nature; understanding useful basic survival skills; personal communication through storytelling; are still available with the help of the internet, via Wikipedia, but this information is now just harder to find but part of a new system of collective intelligence.

Similarly, to the lack of knowledge of basic cooking skills, in previous times automatically passed down through the generations; orientations skills, because of the advancement of technology, i.e. GPS; and craftsmen and hand worker skills, how to build and maintain something.

All this critical knowledge has been lost or misplaced over time, during these "generations of convenience" and mainly because of the advancement of technology. We are no longer taught the basics, which is great if everything goes to plan, but probably, as you are experiencing at this moment, sometimes things just do not go the way we had hoped for. Suddenly we are alone, scared and expected to deal with this new and strange

98

situation; a situation that we have no knowledge or experience in dealing with.

Taking care of ourselves:

Chances are that you are now feeling shit-scared, frustrated, confused or even angry. You want the pain to stop or go away. You are willing to do almost anything to alleviate that pain from this moment, by, for example, using or misusing alcohol, drugs, sex or even food. And indeed, not giving a rat's arse about the expected iron-clad will-power or the lack of it - to accompany you.

Relaxing:

When teaching my students and trainees ... I tell them to breathe, relax and move down from the logic of the brain/head, and begin to live and trust in the heart ... the partly forgotten intuitive part of our consciousness. Relax and know that nothing has gone wrong and that this ... this is just perhaps only a momentary stepping-stone, leading to something new and exciting on the other side of the stream.

Stressed out:

The stressed-out person can experience intimidation by anyone involved or by the stressful circumstance itself. This can be heightened or exacerbated by mental health issues, such as depression, feelings of under-achievement, experiencing peer-group pressure between colleagues or feeling and looking ill or overweight.

Experiencing long-term stress exaggerates the feelings of complete dissatisfaction with him or herself. He is hypersensitive to criticism, which in turn makes him fearful of making new active decisions and even deciding on the most basic and banal things, such as the choice between tea or coffee. This leads to extreme indecisiveness, owing to the fear of getting it wrong (once again). Increasingly, she is trying to rationalise her perfectionism by agreeing with the majority and becoming a yes-sayer more of the time. She also has an air of hostility about her; she is irritable most of the time and highly pessimistic and aggressive towards others who appear weak or those that are making silly mistakes.

Under severe stress, the image of ourselves and others becomes tainted; we generally have lower self-esteem about our behaviour, plus we are incredibly self-critical and negative about our unique place in the world. In general, we measure ourselves by using our perception of what others think about us. This is totally subjective and, most of the time, not even true or accurate.

The positive vision of self:

Having a positive but realistic opinion of one's self-concept is highly influential within the workplace. This self-identity, for example, self-acceptance of ethnicity or religion; self-realisation of academic and work experience; self-construction of gender; self-perspective regarding sexual and gender identity; all make up the more significant you, the image you wish to portray and the way you are perceived at your place of work.

Keeping active:

In the field of neuroscience, and in recent neuroscientific research, it has now becoming increasingly evident that using and training our brains, especially at work, by taking on something new, or planning an exciting project, helps us to keep the onset of dementia at arm's length, and, at the same time, these challenges help to build and create strategies to increase a stronger and more general resilience to the modern killers, i.e. mental stress, fatigue and burnout.

9

SOOTHING WORDS

"History shows us that in in times of people feeling like they are in need of some sort of rebellion or protests, the artists rise because the poetry we create about pain and its relationship to culture in the world beings to soothe and heal people who are feeling confused or afraid."

Lady Gaga

Many people now accept *"struggle"* as a necessary and inevitable part of modern human existence. Whereas in the past, frugality, abstinence and piousness were deemed commendable; now, *struggle* has taken this top-notch place. However, it is essential to realise and remember that struggle through the thought process does not actually exist more than any other thought,

101

such as the feelings of fear, joy or envy. The perceived negative notion of struggle is, in fact, neutral and merely *"a free choice of the mind"* at the moment of thinking and nothing more.

Here are a few more suggestions and soothing words, dealing with the various topics which might affect us during the course of our day, and which might help to solve real problems about living and working in the real world.

Mindfulness and Meditation:

Mindfulness is the opposite of struggle. Although somewhat ineffable and elusive, mindfulness can be seen as a "method of mind relaxation and the relinquishment of mind judgement and control." Primarily, we use our innate ability to consider feelings and actions, in the present continuous moment and go deeper in thought horizontally without going deeper vertically.

Mindful thought can be seen as being a more reliable way of thinking thoughts, something innate and something that we have to reconnect with *if* we are to have more peace of mind. It offers us the ability to consider and think of something in a different, free and positive way.

Over time we have masked our innate qualities and ease of mindfulness. Once we realise this, we only need to slow the train of thought down so that we can board the carriage generally moving in a mindful direction.

Being mindful means that we are checking and observing our thinking throughout our waking hours, by doing those routine things, like eating, breathing, walking, combing our hair, etc. Always repeatedly returning to what our thoughts and experiences in that *"now"* and *"present"* moment in time. Using anything other than the average, uncontrollable thought processes, for example: emotions, feelings, intuition, etc., and in turn hopefully providing us more control and peace of mind when the next stressful event or negative thought occurs. We need to reduce our cognitive thinking so that we can *"hear"* on a deeper level and eventually heal. Therefore, we must re-obtain the right to once again be more selfish and to consider and learn what we truly want and need.

Naturally, as with many other issues discussed in this book, such as: sleep, hydration, nutrition, exercise - being and remaining in an unmindful state in the long-term is not helpful; although finding a holistic level or state of well-being is undoubtedly desirable, it is without question worthwhile. For many, however, some have not reached *"rock bottom"*; some might not be *willing or able* to use what is offered in this book, because it raises childhood trauma or just negative memories of the past. Mindfulness is something that we need to learn, practice, or as stated previously, relearn and reuse daily.

We need to gradually take back control of our thoughts ... without them running ahead **or** remaining in the past. This control of our thinking, striving to remain in the *now* moment, is key to slowing things down. When we are eating, we have to learn to be *fully present* in that eating process or moment; when we are talking with someone, we should be fully there to really listen; when we are drinking coffee, we must take the time to feel the warmth of the water and taste the coffee at the back of our throats.

Meditation is an integral part of being mindful. After regular meditation, there is a definite thickening of three parts of the brain:

- - the hippocampus (responsible for memory and memory retrieval)
- - the Pons, an area of the brain stem accountable for regulatory neurotransmitters production.
- - the TPJ, (temporoparietal junction) being responsible for perspective taking, compassion and empathy.
- - posterior cingulate cortex - responsible for mind wandering and self-actualisation.

There is also, at the same meditative time, a reduction of size and activity of the amygdala the *fight or flight* switch (causing lower rates of anxiety, fear and general worry).

Trauma, Loss and Grief:

After trauma, loss or grief it is normal to have repeated loops of negative thoughts that we know "deep down" do not help us; and taking back "control" of these thoughts, usually takes time, practice and a lot of patience. For many, being fully in charge of our thoughts, similar to those who hear voices from within, is a life-long daily practice. Our job is, whenever possible, to remember that these voices or thoughts are *"real"*, only in the sense that we can understand the words, but believing what these thoughts are saying, especially at heightened and stressful times, is NOT necessarily the absolute or whole truth, nor the best thing for us to hear or to act upon. We have to find a way to become non-attached to our thoughts; together with those past hurts and previous relationships, if we are to be entirely free and progress.

Being active:

Getting out and about in the fresh air or doing some form of exercise is probably the best and easiest way of relativising your exaggerated thoughts or even distracting yourself in conversation with family and friends. When talking with others, we *"block out"* that voice temporarily, as we cannot think two parallel thoughts at the same time. Tell someone trusted how you are feeling. Finding that empathetic person and talking with him or her, will help you realise that you are not alone and that this fear and anxiety is normal and is just part of our human experience; a human experience that gets out of whack from time to time.

Being out in nature, i.e. walking, breathing and exploring unfamiliar places, not only helps to keep our five senses active and curious, but also heightens our higher senses too, and keeps us alert and attentive to all things new, novel and even potentially dangerous. Like drinking a glass of wine which we are unfamiliar with, we pour the wine into a glass, then observe the colour and alcohol (wine legs), after we smell and enjoy the bouquet and finally we taste it ... before swallowing.

We can use other functions of the brain or the senses to assist us in times of stress, anxiety and even trauma. Which at the same time, permits the non-essential negative thoughts to be blocked out temporarily and provides clarity of thought and absolute concentration. With practice, this multi-sensory part of the brain can help with the interconnectivity of different regions of the brain and, as so, promotes spatial cognition: how people learn and use cues from their environment; to determine where they are; to find meaning; to understand place; to find safety and eventually their own way home.

Weight training:

From the age of 40, there is a natural slow, progressive loss of skeletal muscle mass, between 0.5% to 1% per year, meaning that we need to consciously develop muscle mass at around this age. However, regardless of age or physical condition, we need to make time for, and schedule in, a minimum of thirty-minute weight-training routine (alternating with some aerobic training). This activity alone, together with a healthy diet, is sufficient to stave off this loss and will assist in a general feeling of well-being, but especially at times of depression, grief and/or significant change.

Dealing with big issues and events:

As mentioned before, and in the mountain analogy, if we dissect something substantial in front of us, a mountain for example, into smaller more manageable steps or base camps, this can make the perception of the overall ascent much more manageable and undoubtedly less daunting. This is especially helpful when facing a perceived giant step or hurdle. This

106

learned helplessness is a condition in which a person feels a sense of powerlessness or disenfranchisement, arising from some traumatic event or frequent failure and is perhaps the most likely underlying cause of depression.

Becoming more social:

On a more practical note, it might be beneficial to join a club, such as meditation, yoga, Tai Chi or Karate, whereby we are doing something active, being around other people and doing something for our own body and soul.

We must prepare to be part of a new group if we decide to leave our current job or position. Consider if you would prefer to be pushed or leave of your own devices? Your social network, friends and family are incredibly important now and should be tended and cared for, so that there is little or no isolation, loneliness, etc. later.

The quality of the relationship we have with other people is more important than the amount or sum. Remember that what we are experiencing at home or at work, has a direct correlation to *all* the other people in our lives, and the opposite is also true. All energy fields are related and connected to one another and influenced, not only by what we do but also with everyone that we encounter. It will not help our overall being if we are always taking a defensive posture against those who criticise us. Do not argue with others that are in a different place, or have a different mindset to yours, at this moment in time.

Sleep problems:

During some insomniac episodes, it might be beneficial to write down your thoughts and prioritise them by putting them into some sort of order. Once out and on paper, these thoughts then become *"real"*, and this releases them from the repeated loop of nightly inner thought. The next morning, we can then reconsider if these thoughts are *real* or *important* and decide later if a solution and further action is necessary or not. There are many new wake-up lights and alarms available on the market which makes waking up at a regular time, but especially in the winter, more bearable, especially when we are beginning to train the body or change routines.

When we starve the brain of sleep, recent research has indicated that not only are we less concentrated in our waking state, but that it also has a physical effect upon the brain itself, this starts a process of the brain beginning to self-destruct: https://www.newscientist.com.

Getting professional help:

Consider getting professional assistance if you are experiencing severe anxiety or more worry than what you have experienced in the past. Only you can really judge this ... however, as mentioned before, your thinking and judgement might be impaired because of the stress happening to you at this moment.

Depression:

More than cancer, heart disease and car accidents, suicide in the UK is now the major cause of death in men between 20-50 and, as major depression is often associated with suicide and suicidal thoughts, it is crucial to tell a professional how you are feeling and share the thoughts that frequent your mind, especially when experiencing high levels of stress or having symptoms of burnout.

Depression which is generally defined as having long-lasting bouts (lasting at least two weeks) of negative thoughts or thought patterns. This is different, however, from just feeling *a little sad* or having frequent *sad moods*. Whereas feeling a little depressed might be considered "normal", especially after some tragic event or stressful occurrence, having depression, on the other hand, can significantly affect the quality of life on a daily basis; most experience a loss of interest in ordinary things, have a feeling of helplessness and even with life in general.

Although depression is now considered *"treatable"* and is more frequently and openly talked about in society, it must first be appropriately diagnosed, and either some form of speaking therapy or medication or both can then be prescribed. However, depressive symptoms might be caused by other medical or physical issues, such as a vitamin deficiency or an over-active thyroid gland. This highlights the importance of getting professional help early on.

Misuse of alcohol:

The use or misuse of alcohol, in a vain attempt to dull down the powerlessness of high levels of stress and burnout, can not only be a significant long-term causal indicator of depressive bouts or recurrent depressive episodes but can also cause long-term damage and problems with the major organs of the body.

Working from home:

As mentioned before, it is not only the lack of exercise which can have a detrimental effect on those people who experience burnout or are stressed at work, but the general office environment is also crucial. Companies can save significantly by reducing the number of square metres for office space required, especially so in big cities, when it is deemed that an employee *does not need* an actual office or desk to work from. This lack of being part of the dominant hive structure, or the typical working office environment, can negatively affect those employees who are generally on the road most of the time; those who have no designated office space, but are using hot-desking; and those that work from home on most days, are those that are particularly affected by this form of extreme optimisation and exclusion.

Being made redundant or bowing out:

With redundancy, dismissal, voluntary quitting or leaving your present working environment there will always be a certain degree of change, plus the subtle emotions involved; missing the colleagues; missing the routine, and the act of commuting to and from work. This workplace isolation and disruption of routine can also cause social isolation, together with experiencing similar emotions, such as with grief and/or bereavement.

As previously mentioned, it is essential to get the right level of support, to combat possible loneliness, confusion and depression, after having left work and moving on. Keeping a good check of those feelings, emotions and thoughts are paramount, together with frequently questioning what you consider to be *true* or *real*. Learning to find that "belonging feeling" at work or within your own community is incredibly important, regardless if you are *"staying"* or *"moving on"* to pasture's new.

Nutritional Flexibilism:

Regularly changing the brands and foodstuffs might not only be a wise but a healthy choice, as it is not only to keep your diet from becoming boring and bland but to also avoid the consumption of contaminated or substandard ingredients used in its production or in the way it has been stored. By exchanging these products regularly with similar brands and products, this helps to balance out the bad with the good.

Supplements and Vitamins:

If possible, eat *proper* food and not the supplements on the market. Taking dietary supplements and additional vitamins are generally not necessary for the average person, if that same person eats a balanced diet, despite what the hype or media are telling us. As mentioned before, there are, however, certain things that the body needs, but cannot produce itself, i.e. Omega 6.

The marketing, supply and consumption of synthetic dietary and nutritional food supplements have become big business over the years. Whereas adding extra protein to your diet for muscle-gain can sometimes be advantageous, most other supplements and vitamins consumed are not even absorbed and are swiftly flushed through the body, together with those who have kidney disease and/or those taking certain medications.

The current trend of mega-dosing or taking high doses of, for example, B12 (essential for red blood cell development and the nervous system on the whole) or Vitamin D (important, not only for bone health, but also has preventative qualities, such as being an anti-inflammatory agent, for muscle function and even for assisting in general brain health), is not generally recommended or advisable without a doctor recommending such supplements for a specific problem or ailment.

So, if by eating natural foodstuffs, a good balance of consuming leafy green vegetables, fresh fruit, proteins, etc. and getting out more, instead of continually consuming synthetic vitamins or supplements, this, in turn, should generally be sufficient to counteract most vitamin deficiencies found. And if it is vital to have a good general environment of the brain, together with its interconnectivity of the neurotransmitters or synapses (which are responsible for all brain functions, such as: thoughts, emotions, feelings, etc.), then we need to make sure that the brain has the best possible environment it can have.

Although it sounds simple, perhaps too simplistic and probably dull, recent research is still showing that the Mediterranean diet, containing lots of leafy green foods, appears to be the best for overall health, but especially for the environment of our gut, together with longevity and even improves better cognition, connected with the health of the brain's functions.

The organic and regional alternative:

Genuinely organic food not only looks and tastes far better than its mass produced and sub-standardised counterpart; but the carbon footprint of the produce generally has less of an impact on the environment; and finally, fresh produce, sourced from the region where it was grown, helps to keep intact the freshness and taste, between the field and plate.

Organic meats and other products such as eggs, cheese, etc. although slightly more expensive, offer a somewhat more humane alternative to using animals as food, as compared to that of the vegan and vegetarian ideologies.

The quantity of protein might be limited to offer a healthier lifestyle, with approximately 100 grams of fresh, high-quality protein eaten each day, either meat (chicken or fish) or cheese and/or eggs. This could then be divided up into smaller meals and should be sufficient to assist with the development of muscle-mass, which is essential for a healthy body.

When we overload our body with stress, but especially the digestive system, toxins and unwanted by-products cannot be discharged or replaced quickly enough by healthy cells. Free radicals are the toxic by-products of metabolism in the cells and attack essential macromolecules in the body, and this can eventually lead to significant damage to our cells.

Although the body needs a healthy balance between free radicals and antioxidants, if these free radicals begin to over-whelm the body a process known as oxidative stress, which can eventually alter the DNA, can lead to and cause the onset of a number of major human diseases. Therefore, it is essential to eat more of certain nutrients (antioxidants) and to keep a good healthy balance of food, to assist and deal with this oxidative stress, when it occurs or gets out of balance.

Being adaptable and flexible:

Life chances, together with the dynamic and hectic progression of modern society, will undoubtedly mean that most employees will now have to be more amenable to survive and thrive. It will probably mean that we will no longer be able to continue with our original and designated ideal profession or the well-intentioned and planned career first thought out. Especially for an incumbent older male employee, modern day life, both in society but especially at work, is full of many stressful new situations and to successfully survive this changing area we need to quickly modify and adapt our attitudes, both in terms of our professional, but also that of our personal and family lives.

The older we get, the harder it is to accept change. The more willing and prepared an employee is to adapt and continue on within the company, with a possible new proposed future direction being offered, just means that, despite being at an older age, he or she is showing commitment, loyalty and still willing to adapt.

For the benefit of the whole organisation and team, it is vital that the younger, more youthful employees, strive to understand the thinking and philosophy behind those that have worked in an "old style" type of workplace.

The older members of the team, the former gerontocracy (those who generally have large monthly bills (mortgages, loans, etc.), and those who still need a certain amount of financial

113

security), often still find it hard to fully accept these changes. They also believe deep-down that seniority, experience and knowledge, still deserve a higher salary, deference, promotion and ultimately more respect.

The more willing, prepared and adaptable an older employee is, for example, the request to relocate with the company, the easier it will be to truly accept this newly proposed personal future career path and, at the same time, indicates a continuing positive commitment to the organisation.

This willingness to adapt, instead of being anti or slowing things down, indicates to the company and the team, that an older employee is happy to stay abreast of any new techno-logical advances or changes to the mission statements being implemented; such as, the enrolment in the many retraining initiatives or completing any relevant training or upskilling courses being offered, to ultimately obtain the necessary and vital qualifications needed for the future.

Although this might pose a few problems in the beginning, perhaps being the most mature person or student in the classroom, this new learning and continuation of personal education, significantly helps us to, not only keep the brain active and the synaptics firing but can also reduce the chances of dementia later on in life.

Your thinking and behaving:

Similar to the Placebo effect, and the self-fulfilling prophecy (believing something and making it so in our reality) can actually help us stay young and healthy. Just by thinking less about illness and more about having a healthy, energetic body, together with the way we behave, by keeping alert and interested in learning new things, significantly slows the ageing process down. It is also important to remember that, we are what we think; we are what we eat, and we are what we say. So, it is vital to choose our thoughts, foods and words wisely.

Our perception of the world, our world-view (Weltanschauung), is fundamentally linked to the way we see and believe the world to be. If we are taught something at an early age and think it is *true*, we will accept this to be "as given" and truthful in nature. This truthful reality or paradigm, however, is purely subjective and transient. Despite this, this is still how we give meaning to our lives and the world, regardless of circumstance and situation. With this truth, when combined with the truths of others, it becomes our perceptive reality and can ultimately lead to action or non-action. It is this self-efficacy which can assist us in the way we deal with the long-term coping measures, but also our general ability to start and complete tasks.

The unrealistic but expected norm:

Whereas before, and as an exception to the rule, the model worker, was being asked to multi-task for most of the working day, together with the expectations of being and showing "presence" and "interconnectivity" to the call of all things related to work, even after the typical working day had ended. This has now, however, changed significantly and has become the rule and part of the regular run of things. This is not only unrealistic and unattainable in the long-term, but also detrimental to physical health, causing untold and unnecessary stress, fatigue and eventual burnout. It is feeding an insatiable monster; a monster that feeds on productivity and optimisation and will, however, never be satisfied; wanting more and more until breaking the camel's back with a single straw or the heightened expectation of keeping an ever-increasing number of plates spinning at the same time.

Recent research has shown that giving just one ear to a telephone conversation or being in a meeting at the end of the day while updating our to-do list or thinking about something else work-related, is basically a waste of time for all concerned. Doing whatever we are doing, with 100% dedication and full concentration, even if this might take a little longer, is generally better for all concerned. Really listening to what is being said, and replying after really hearing the question, is being respectful to the other person, regardless if speaking to a colleague or client.

Whereas lapses of concentration are common, especially at the end of the working day, and perhaps deemed as being disrespectful; telling the truth and being honest is always a better way of communicating and doing business in general.

Empowerment:

Although we have acknowledged and understood that if the future of worker's empowerment is to be kept at the same or even an increased level, it is the job of the managers and senior managers to encourage the willing participation and collaboration of their teams, thus offering true empowerment in return for ongoing effectiveness and efficiency.

To avoid the negativity of being bloody-minded or stubborn at work, together with the withholding of knowledge and expertise, because of an increase in the engagement of work intensification, an employer will have to offer a more direct and concrete connection between having significant rewards and benefits, thus leading to a freer sharing of valuable experience and knowledge amongst its staff.

Although being present in the workplace can have certain positive benefits, for example, collegiality, the sharing of knowledge and expertise, etc., when working from home the

116

employee has the freedom to decide for themselves how and when they intend to complete the assigned daily work tasks. It is essential that the mature manager learns to have more trust, almost a laissez-faire attitude, of letting loose of the reins for a while and without "supervision" as a method of control, and ultimately allowing the employee to do his or her job.

The increase of entrepreneurship, but especially for those older or those who find themselves stuck within the poverty trap or work-poverty, has resulted in offering a doable alternative for coping with the negative feelings of disenchantment, disempowerment and disfranchisement, and, ultimately, a way to fight for and to take back control of one's life.

If we equate, living in a capitalist (neoliberal) society, with playing a game of Monopoly, but playing the game with a set of significant disadvantages right from the start, for example: the means of the acquisition of wealth, gaining capital and material things are not realistically achievable; or having an unjust and ever-changing set of rules to play by; or if it is not possible to win, even by following and playing by the rules; or being excluded from taking part in the actual game; then we have to ask ourselves the question: *Why play the game at all?*

This paradoxical situation and frustration can only lead to three possible alternatives: Change the game (revolution); stop playing the game (relocate), or accept the status quo (shut the fuck up) and lump it. *Decisions? Decisions? Decisions?*

Remote Working:

Similarly, being forced to work remotely or from outside the typical working environment (home office), by using the latest technological advancements available, such as digitalisation of files and data (Big Data), teleconferencing, etc., many employees are still not fully experiencing the real "empowerment" promised to them. This is mainly because of their inability to "switch-off" from the hive; the 24/7 expectations; the hectic mentality of the modern work culture; and their failure to challenge this control structure.

The amount of money that it is possible to earn is generally dependent and linked to the number of hours we are expected to be present at our place of work. However, as in former times, it was important for the employer to keep the amount of money low so that the factories could keep on operating and producing. So, if the wages were too high employees would only work enough to satisfy their own needs and then take the rest of the time off to spend the money and relax.

This has now markedly changed, mainly because of significant technological advances, but also with that many jobs are being done by machines and with companies having a vastly reduced number of workers. To boot, there has also recently been a lot of information (and stigmatisation) about having a universal basic income, giving each citizen in society enough money to live, with no strings attached and not related to work. Self-Realisation? The ability to follow one's dreams or passions? We will have to wait and see.

Similarly, with the agile or gig economies, work that can be done on a temporary, freelance or contractual basis, and at the same time, giving greater freedom (working when needed) and working for multiple employers at the same time, there are also some major financial concerns regarding the financial security and flexibility with these models of work.

The major problem with this agile economy is that one can never leave work. As mentioned before, with the onset of the First Industrial Revolution, workers were expected to come to the big cities and become part of the workforce, so that they were in a convenient position to that of the factory. With the onset of the Fourth Industrial Revolution this has been seen to move back out and away from the office (the modern-day factory) and dispersed out; anywhere other than in an expensive office-block or open office, meaning that, on the one hand, one can never literally leave work (mentally/consciously) because of technological and communicative advances, but on the other hand, being excluded from the hive and the beneficial social aspects of office life and work.

Self-efficacy:

To be genuinely efficacious (how well we can carry out specific actions and deal with complicated life situations) we are going to need, not only our wits about us (being able to cope for long periods) but also have the best possible physical condition for our bodies.

This self-efficacy looks at challenges (our health, thoughts, nutrition, etc.) as something that needs to be mastered (fight) rather than something to be avoided (flight). Being confident at our core has shown to be hugely important when looking at performance at work and ultimately with leading a successful life.

We have previously discussed the importance and usefulness of generational observation and the positive outcomes we can achieve by having and doing this. This assists too, not only on our ability to survive and progress; by learning from others (imitation and modelling); but also, by considering the social impact and experience of our cognitive patterns of thought development.

The Placebo effect, together with self-efficacy and the self-fulfilling prophecy, are all parts of a new type of skillset, where both novelty and curiosity act as a method of acceptance and tolerance. By working together, we can use the combined experience and the dynamic new fresh ideas to promote a collective intelligence to take everyone, including the organisation, to the next level.

10

MEDITATION - OR JUST QUIETENING THE MIND

"Dedicating some time to meditation is a meaningful expression of caring for yourself that can help you move through the mire of feeling unworthy of recovery. As your mind grows quieter and more spacious, you can begin to see self-defeating thought patterns for what they are, and open up to other, more positive options."

Sharon Salzberg

You have probably heard many people talk about the benefits of meditation, so why then, do most people refuse to even start to meditate? Meditation has still got a slightly esoteric bitter taste in most people's mouths, but especially those rational people within the business community. Although there have been several famous CEOs who use and swear by it, it is still on the fringes or margins of what is considered to be *normal.*

If we consider just quietening the mind, instead of using the word meditation, this practise then becomes normal and more acceptable to the broader society. This is similar to the title and profession "life coach" in the early 2000s; whereby this label of *life coach* was not at all taken seriously by many at the time, and even questioned its relevance in our private and business lives.

Consider my favourite shirt; a dark green Camel Active cotton shirt, it is something which I feel that I look smart and professional in when teaching, and it feels "right" on my body. However, take this same green shirt and let someone else wear it; chances are, not everyone is going to feel comfortable in it: its colour, its fit (too large or too small); its material and feel; etc. etc. Comparable with teaching or coaching, one size *does not fit* everyone; nor should it. There are many methods, perspectives and plenty of individual teachers and coaches out there. Most important is that you discover what best suits you and yours.

Meditation is just the same. Some people swear by TM (Transcendental Meditation); others find chanting: "Nam Myoho Renge Kyo", practised by the Nichiren Buddhists, to be the ultimate answer; still others use the gracefulness and slowness of the forms of the Chinese Qi Gong orTai Chi (improving posture, balance and breath); or others just enter a church, synagogue or mosque and find that inner peace; or just even praying at home before sleep. All of these methods just slow down our minds and allows that "inner intuitive peace" to wash over our consciousness for a while. However, mindfulness (as a practice) and meditation are both slowly becoming part of the acceptable face of modern business, and are increasingly being taught in some stress and time management courses now.

Probably the most straightforward form of quietening the mind is to take a walk, preferably in nature, perhaps a park or anywhere outside where there are not that many people. Otherwise find a quiet place inside, where you feel safe and will not be disturbed for about 20 minutes; put on some loose-fitting clothing, sit on a chair, or on the floor upon a cushion. Close your eyes and just relax and breathe deeply. Your mind, especially if you are sad, frustrated, angry, stressed, etc., will start to be heard through your thoughts. This is your reasoning, trying to find a solution for your current problem. With no struggle ... just *allow and accept* this voice to be. The more that you fight against this voice, the further away you become from being mindful and finding that quiet gap or place between thoughts.

Think solely and consciously about your breathing, the inhalation and the exhalation, and how this *feels* in your upper body. We could count our breaths if the noise of our own thoughts are too dominant or incessant. This counting has a similar effect by those who use and enjoy chanting or saying a prayer. Remember that, while we are chanting; saying a prayer; walking; or moving through the different forms of Tai Chi; there is less of a chance that that voice, in our heads, can take dominance over our momentary perception of the world via thought.

If there is a constant noise in the room, perhaps the heating system, or some stable buzzing from an electrical appliance, concentrate on that noise. This concentration will, not only distract you from this voice for moments in time but will also offer you an apparent respite and clarity from that voice of thought.

123

When sitting there in meditation, try not to move if possible; avoid wanting to scratch that itch; or even fall asleep - something that happens to people who are beginning the meditation process and those who have been sleeping poorly or insufficiently because of stress in their lives.

Quietening the mind in the meditative and mindfulness process is something to be practised and learned. Even those that have been doing it for some time, still find that remaining in that *"quiet place"*, for long periods, is never easy and always dependent on a whole range of other things that are happening in their lives outside that space of meditation. However, these quiet moments will generally increase with practice, together with the amount of time and intensity that we can "sit" and just "be" in the moment.

Ideally, it would be sufficient to sit and just be in meditation for about 15-20 minutes a day. When and where you do this is dependent on your own circumstance, but generally, doing this first thing in the morning is best. Similar to lifting weights or going for a jog, spending time in the morning meditating, means that whatever else happens on that day, we will have achieved something for our own well-being and nothing then can take this away from us.

Take the next ten minutes to just ... *be*. Set a timer for 10 minutes, then put this book or your tablet down and just switch off and be in the moment. Thoughts will come and go, positive and negative, this is normal and should be expected. Every time a thought arrives at the fore of your consciousness, **do not** try to fight or judge the feeling, instead just allow these thoughts to exist. These thoughts are instinctual, healthy and ultimately there to help us. However, we have to realise that sometimes, our thoughts are kicking in and are in fact, harming us, instead of protecting us, from potentially stressful and life-threatening situations.

These negative thought patterns have been attacked from within and are now, for the most part ... *corrupt*, and serving little or no actual use or purpose. They are more than likely no longer serving you or even useful, and we have to now realise and accept this fact; not on a logical level, but on an emotional one. After acknowledging the negative thought, allow it to be and then waft it away ... the way you would waft away a butterfly from your forearm on a summer's day.

Before turning the page ... take 10 minutes to just be ...

11

FINDING YOUR PASSION

"My mission in life is not merely to survive, but to thrive; and to do so with some passion, some compassion, some humour, and some style."

Maya Angelou

Our lives are divided into three main categories: the past, the present and the future. If we are to make the best of our total life circumstance, we need to take into consideration all three states equally. We should be able to learn from the past, although not dwell there, in some nostalgic and idealistic dream-state; we should plan and consider the future, but remain flexible, heading only in a general direction of the flow of things and always be open for changes, diversions and possible adventures; and lastly, we should occasionally review that critical state, that being our present moment, by using a detailed review or audit, both are integral when in the process of working with a great coach in the modern era.

No longer is the coach there just to inspire or instruct, nor just passively watch from the sidelines. Gone are the days when the sole role of the coach was only to mentor. She is not even there to advise or give guidance. She is now, however, mainly there as a stable, reliable and trustworthy companion; asking pertinent questions at the appropriate times; probing us to answer our own unique questions; and ultimately there to help us select the best path possible; from an infinite multitude of trodden and unique paths.

As mentioned briefly before, Joseph Campbell's notion of the "Hero's Journey" or what others have called the monomyth, describes a tale in which the hero sets out on a beckoning adventure (life) and is asked to partake in several stages or challenges (problems) along the way until, finally, returns home changed and enlightened (happiness).

Campbell divides this journey into three acts or significant parts: The Departure; the Initiation; and finally, the Return, and within these 3 acts, there are the 17 stages or sub-stages. Throughout modern and ancient history, we can find many examples of distinguished people undertaking this journey, such as: Christ, Gandhi, Buddha, together with the classics, such as Plato's Simile of the Cave, Lord of the Rings and even very recently, Luke Skywalker in Star Wars.

Listed below are Campbell's seventeen steps. Consider now for yourself, which act are you presently living in? What challenges are you currently facing? What can we learn or understand about past adverse events? What might make our present situation - together with our possible future paths -

appear brighter or even more positive?

Departure:

1. You are requested to take part in an adventure or significant challenge.

2. You try to ignore or decline the call.

3. You get a helper or an assistant with specialised knowledge, who acts as your personal protector and aid.

4. You start the journey and leave the safety and security of the tribe or harbour.

5. Final separation; you cut off all possible options of returning by burning the bridges behind you.

Initiation:

6. You are set a series of tests (generally three) to check your transformative agility.

7. The final test with the meeting of the Goddess.

8. You become tempted by some desire and consider leaving your quest.

9. You must be challenged and initiated by something that has ultimate power, but you still have to find faith and start to believe.

10. You now know that you have enlightenment and can continue on with the hardest part of the quest.

11. You get the ultimate goal that you set out for.

Return:

12. You may not want to return to the real world and share your bounty.

13. Either escape or go freely with your treasure with possible similar dangers on the return journey.

14. If weakened by the quest, we need someone to assist us in returning with the treasure.

15. Retaining the knowledge learned throughout the quest and the consideration of how to share this knowledge with others.

16. Mastering both the spiritual and material dynamics of the world.

17. Once mastery is achieved, the fear of death or loss is no longer significant; this allows for ultimate freedom, together with accepting all change; and not regretting the woes of the past.

For a more detailed explanation of these stages, here is a link to Wikipedia: https://en.m.wikipedia.org/wiki/Hero%27s_journey.

When reading a book or watching a film, we could at the onset take a quick sneak peek to the end and spoil the carefully creative storyline which the author has meticulously prepared for us.

Gaze, with inquisitive eyes, at your complete life; like the pages of a well-read or dog-eared book. We started out incredibly helpless and needy, knowing very little, but with ample amounts of curiosity and stamina. Over time, and within the many unique chapters, we have found out more about who we are; experienced many challenges; laughed and cried; met interesting and conflictual people, who have ultimately made us into that person, who smiles back at us in the mirror each morning.

If we could genuinely accept, beyond a shadow of a doubt, that by missing our boat; or taking a wrong path; or making a bad decision, previously in the past; that all these supposed "mistakes", were merely only a small part of our intended and natural storyline; and that nothing had gone wrong; would it then be possible to relax more of the time; enjoy the spectacular and unfolding landscape; and ultimately be more curious and less frightened about what the future holds?

If we knew whole-heartedly that another boat was just about to dock at our harbour; that a similar path, leading to the same or a better destination, was just around the next bend or corner; and that ultimately, there were no real "bad" decisions made in the past; would this make your life easier and more worth living? Just by accepting that those previous perceived mistakes were more about *learning new things* and gaining valuable experiences about life; and that those supposedly missed boats, wrong paths and errors were all part of the tapestry of life; would this knowledge now make you feel more confident about those previous decisions? And would you now be more willing and courageous to try out new things in the future?

So, if we could acknowledge and heartedly accept that our own past, present and future lives, are akin to that of the character in the book or on that journey of heroes, would then the undertaking of that said journey now be more comfortable to start or continue?   And that setting out on that next adventurous journey would, by the end of the story, all turn out just fine.   And that you would return safe and sound, after having succeeded in the many exciting challenges set and posed against you? And the untold adventures which you will experience; together with the gifts and treasures found *en route*, would the undertaking of that said future journey, now be more a walk in the park, or at least much easier than previously thought?

Know and fully accept that where you are ... is just ... *where you are*! It is not wrong, and nothing has actually gone astray.

You may feel that you have left your path or missed your boat because of how you are feeling, or by a series of recent events and situations, but everything is working out for you, at this very moment. It is only your current or momentary time-line upon an ever-changing stage, which is, nothing more than, the neutral story of your life.

12

STOP DIGGING YOUR HOLE

"It is a good thing to follow the
First Law of Holes: if you are in
one, stop digging."
Denis Healey

De omnibus dubitandum, everything must be questioned or doubted, and with these wise words of wisdom, we have now momentarily (perhaps through meditation) ceased from digging that perfectly sculptured hole and stopped decorating and ornating it with delicate objects and countless riches. This respite allows us to stop, and realise and remember that ...

"A hole is ... just a hole."

and this hole is, more than likely, presently preventing you from seeing the whole, ultimate and absolute truth and reality about you; yourself; and your life in general.

Your inner being; the real you; your soul, if you prefer, does, in fact, know exactly who you are; where you have been; and where you intend going, if only given a chance to reconnect once more, to that natural, ever present and available energy and place. If, after getting this far through the book, you are still not totally convinced, then do me a favour and take a weekend off; just be patient and listen; without struggle and with little or no expectation; and wait for that certain something to tap you on the shoulder. Just listen and wait for the synchronicities and serendipities to surprise, delight and enlighten you. Joseph Campbell talked about a unique door opening just for you and no one else. Similarly, we should be searching for that easy path of least resistance, leading to an ultimate "inner knowing" or peace of mind.

In the meantime, be particularly patient and kind to yourself. This resistance to change, plus the perceived choices and freedoms involved in this change, has progressively become the benchmark or the norm. It will undoubtedly take some time, for that built-up momentum and energy, to slow down enough, for you to once again truly regain your balance; and to finally move in a new, but different and positive direction.

When we have a lot of stress at work, the primary emotions experienced is that of an overwhelming feeling of panic and general helplessness. We know and feel that we are heading towards an unknown and dangerous waterfall; being caught up in the flow of that river, and mostly having little or no power to change direction. Similarly, envision having a train carriage in the middle of two identical locomotives, each pulling in the opposite direction. As long as both locomotives continue to tug and pull, little movement or progression happens, with the exception of causing a lot of stress, heat and strain on the carriage in the middle. This is precisely how we feel when we are enduring long-term stress; having worry and anxiety at work, or just being ill or under the weather. We are resisting being ripped or torn apart from our true selves. We are being tortured deciding between continuing on with our stressful workload and being loyal to the company, the colleagues and completing our workload before the deadline; rather than considering what is best for **us**; our own health and well-being; and knowing intuitively when to stop and take some time off to truly recover and find balance.

Regardless of what we do, always remember that we are upon our unique and enlightened journey or path and, as so, we have to just consciously take a different perspective of it. At the same time, we have to decide if we want to do this sooner or later, and view our temporary situation either through positive or negative eyes? We can either do this willingly or not? Now or later? Irrespective if you think that your intended boat has now left the harbour, the truth is … there is an armada of other similar ships sailing every hour. Our choice is to choose which one and when; perfect free will and perfect harmony being presented and offered to us in this and every moment.

Once we recall our true potential, past experiences no longer have any real significance or relevance to our *now*. We are not the same person we were ten years ago or even, for that matter, this morning. Each morning when we awaken, we are that new person. Celebrate and acknowledge that new persona and relax into that new role with a new, positive and dynamic potentiality. We no longer need forgiveness or even need to punish ourselves about past events. We are free and have done nothing wrong … except travel along our own *intended* path.

Especially in times of extreme stress, and as mentioned previously, the main concern with using thought, as a way of problem-solving, is that firstly, we can only think one thought at a time, and secondly, we cannot consciously stop ourselves from thinking something, such as: "I am no longer going to think about the stress at my job".

Each of us has lived time in the past, but this does not necessarily need to be our accompanying companion for the present or future. Be ready and prepared to travel light and at a moment's notice, but perhaps more importantly, depart without *"Fear"* and *"Anxiety"* as your negative companions; choosing your close and trusted friends, *"Ease"* and *"Flexibility"* to accompany you, instead.

Every time we had a thought or made a decision in the past and regretted it, we learned something from this time and experience. If we consider this merely as a learning experience and perhaps something positive, then we can use this, at a future date, to assist us in removing or diverting around similar obstacles along our path.

Our true nature, once acknowledged and really listened to, remains incredibly forgiving and continues to offer us signposts and suggestions towards our future, and with never a harsh word or reprimand when we decide **not** to listen or follow its instructions. It soothes us towards the next newness; it coaxes us with kind words, and our true nature continuously whispers to us subtle and clear instructions.

When we know what we honestly **do not** want, we certainly know, at the same time, what we ultimately **do** want. And all this quality advice comes for free and is very intuitive, once we slow down and learn to really *listen*. It is calling us forward; baby steps to begin with; and then more substantial and significant stepping-stones to tread upon in the future.

When we feel guilt, remorse or experience negative emotions about something we have done or said to someone in the past, realise that the only reason we are having these negative thoughts or feelings is that our natural *self* is experiencing and thinking the exact opposite. This is the reason why we feel so bad after the fact, and our natural state "*knows*" that this is not who we really are.

When we are unhappy, feeling frustrated or just having negative thoughts and emotions, then we are not fulfilling our true potential of who we really are and not, at the same time, completing or accomplishing our sole reason for being here. We are being less than authentic, and this is why it feels so disingenuous, fake and mostly just plain wrong.

Shit is always going to happen; this is normal and part of our continuously changing lives. The quicker we realise and accept this, the faster and more comfortable we will obtain what we truly want and, more importantly, become that happier, more contented and authentic person.

We have discussed many issues and also talked at length about a multi-pronged action plan in this book. Similar to riding a horse, there are many things that we have to concentrate on and do at the same time: i.e. keeping control of our posture; using enough, but not too much attention on the reins; remain up to date with the modern trends and technologies; looking forward rather than looking down; and perhaps most importantly, remembering to breathe, enjoy the ride and try to be more confident in our approach to all things.

However, if for example we only reduce the amount of alcohol (which is incredibly essential on its own), but continue to overeat, then this is not going to help our overall and long-term advancement. This is true of the many issues discussed within this book and, as so, we need to decide to make an immediate change and take massive action all at the same time, which, I realise is, no easy feat.

However, at the same time, we should not be too hard on ourselves. We are, but merely human, and as so, quite fallible. Do not beat yourself up when you fall off the wagon; just pick yourself up after a short time; brush off that dirt; get back on the wagon and continue *that unique journey of yours.*

Detach yourself from your electronic devices regularly, but especially from all social media. You are trying to wean yourself off from this habit, so once in an hour is sufficient to check messages and catch up. Choose a quiet time, perhaps between 9pm and 7am. Put your mobile device on "flight mode" when you need to get something done, so that you will not be distracted or seduced into going off on a time consuming and wasteful tangent.

Realise that you are just getting in your own way most of the time. Listen to your instincts and acknowledge your cravings. If you are thirsty drink water; if you have cravings for coffee, alcohol or sugary things, then decide if an alternative is available or if you can have something less addictive and slightly healthier.

People do not seem to care anymore (see additional chapter after this one) about other people most of the time, let alone animal welfare, homelessness, inflation, poverty, social justice, etc. Most people are just caught up in their own thoughts and problems, and you are further on down the list of things to be acknowledged or considered necessary.

Do not be too saddened or frustrated, for example, by the major manufacturers trying to pull the wool over our eyes and the eyes of the consumer by, for example, subtly making the actual product smaller, but selling the product to us for the same price, hoping that we will not notice. Remember that financial elites, big companies and corporations are not actually there to solve any national or international problems of the world, but instead only thinking about making and selling its own products and services cheaper than that of its individuals competitors - nothing more and nothing less. Know that, generally, big businesses are only interested in the highest price that we are willing to pay at the checkout for their products and ultimately to line their own pockets and the pockets of their shareholders.

Notice, remember and boycott these products and companies, if and when possible. When we boycott these products enough, big business manufacturers will eventually decide not to use sub-standard industrial ingredients to make their products; exploit its own workforce; mistreat the animals used in production; or mislead the consumer regarding advertising, marketing, labelling and packaging. Then and only then, will our trust and loyalty for the company, its brands and products fully return. Until then, it is undoubtedly the role and responsibility of the elected government, those who we pay our taxes to, to regulate and control these large companies, with consumer laws, employment regulations and food safety guidelines, for our protection.

Task 4:
Now that you have almost completed this book, once again,

write a very simple story about **where you are** and **where you would like to be** in one year. Consider at least two different paths or alternatives (three or four would be even more advantageous). Consider reframing something which you consider to be hard, impossible or even slightly harmful in nature. What can we learn from this experience? Why might this be something positive for us in the future? When writing this story, remain flexible and adaptable in the outcome. Then compare this to your original account in Chapter One. Consider now, what has changed?

As mentioned previously, it is crucial that we do something positive for ourselves, by building and practising that cognitive resonance, but especially if we are currently experiencing significant stress or in a depressive state. For ten or twenty minutes, take some time out daily and watch or read anything positive, such as the many TED Talks - https://www.ted.com - available on the internet. Listen and learn from the experiences of others, by perhaps drawing from their knowledge and consider if we could change something similar in our own lives.

Think carefully about the following questions: Are you happy with your whole self? Would you prefer to be someone waking up each morning feeling relaxed and looking forward to the challenges of the day? Or someone that has not slept well, tossing and turning all night, and someone who has not had enough sleep?

Start off by physically writing some sort of daily Gratitude Diary or Journal. Do this physically, rather than digitally if possible, because then it becomes real, in the sense that we can feel the paper and hold the pen in our hand. A place where we can write down freely about just "One Thing", "One Event", or "One Situation" that we enjoyed or experienced on that day. Perhaps a smile from another commuter or someone helped us in the office or a great tasting biscuit brought in by a colleague. These small notes or entries subtly change our practised negativity into something more positive. Important is that we start to move away from seeing our current workplace and lives in a negative light. This negativity bias, moving away from a place of negativity and seeing more of the benefits and positive attributes of our work, is key to having a more enjoyable life both at work or working remotely from some place else.

Accept that the circumstances of our lives are not likely to dramatically change today, tomorrow or even in the near future. However, what we *can* change, and with immediate effect and with a little practice is, that we always have the power to change or adjust our thoughts and the way we think about our circumstances and situations; thus, and more importantly, giving us enough power to make things change from within. Being patient and doing this regularly causes a different, more positive, vibration to radiate out from us. Our steps will seem lighter; we will shine more, without having anything having changed physically in our environment; and other people will start to notice and perhaps comment on this new way of *being in the world*.

And finally, the next time you contemplate digging an excellent new hole for yourself, a hole that eventually you are going to be scrambling out of later, think carefully if: *this action and energy is really necessary, beneficial or the best use of your time?*

I would love to hear your comments regarding this book -
https://amzn.to/2Jclatg

Why we should care

Writing this book has been a long and personal journey and is set down, either on paper or as an e-book, and presented to you as just an alternative to how you have been managing, both your life at the moment and that of your past. If you are unhappy with your lot or looking for something markedly more and new, then consider the information in this book as *just* an alternative, especially if you have had little or no success doing it the usual or old-fashioned way. I have outlined many scenarios and raised thoughts and questions about what exists and what could or might be changed. The primary purpose of this book is dealing with the customarily considered and anticipated activities of life, not only within the working environment but also, and probably more important, your private and personal thoughts and lives.

Always remember that the way we think, together with our behaviour, is probably the most crucial factor in living a peaceful and happy life. Intuitively, we know **what is** and **what is not** right for us at any given moment in time; providing we have the necessary "quietness" and "peace of mind" to really listen, hear and truly understand. Just knowing the statistical facts about life, is apparently insufficient to stop most of us from chain smoking, binge drinking and doing all those things that we *know* are bad for us, especially when we are stressed out, depressed or anxious. For example, the fact that in the year 2050 there are going to be an estimated 20 million people in Europe suffering from Dementia; yet, are we willing to do something *now* to prevent us becoming part of this statistic? Instead of playing this health roulette game with our lives, perhaps we need to consider those more profound, more holistic recommendations and scientific suggestions in this book, to truly live our lives; to be happy; and to be really contented. It all boils down to our ability to not only read the words within this book but to internalise them and use them, so that long-term change may occur.

As Seneca wrote: *"True happiness is ... to enjoy the present, without anxious dependence on the future."* Being in "the now" always means accepting the past and being excited about the challenges and changes of the future, and as so, it is key to living a balanced and happy life.

Consider the messages and information in this book now. What are you going to take along with you for the ride? What is new, and what could you do differently next time you are confronted with a stressful situation?

I would certainly request that you do this transformational change with the help of a good or great coach. The coach does not need to have the same maturity or expertise as you. This does not make him *less* helpful in your progression, but can, in fact, be a benefit to you, by being able to take a neutral and unbiased view of your current events.

What the excellent coach should have, is heaps of curiosity; an attentive listening ear; and an observant, watchful eye. He or she should not tell you what to do, but rather be able to ask pertinent questions at the right time and to help you move forward when change is required.

Within the twelve chapters of this book, we looked at what we have; what we want; and then went on to investigate how to prepare our body and mind for this unique journey in detail.

Consider your work and life as a game; realise the importance in understanding that we are *merely* players in an ongoing team and storyline. Why do we play a game? Because we enjoy the pleasure and challenge of the experience. We will not always win, but that is part of playing the game. We will always learn from the experience and hopefully, have fun at the same time. This is something that we could not experience if we were alone and solitudal. With this experience, we need to look at what worked, what did not, and what we can learn for the next round or future experience.

In Chapter Three, we talked about the quote from a famous London painter ... that painter was my father. I do not remember much of what my father told me, but he often reminded me of what is and what is not essential in life. Not only was he my father, but a painter and decorator ... and this book is dedicated to him and his memory.

"You're a long time dead."

"You are a long time dead." Eddie Birks

I hope that you experienced and enjoyed the warmth of this book. Use the information wisely; put into practice some or all of the ideas and techniques offered; and, if possible, pass this knowledge on to someone you think can really hear the message.

To summarise, having quality of life; the hope to stay cognitively alert, with good physical health and having loving people around us, is far more critical than having fabulous houses, lots of money in your bank account or even living an affluent lifestyle. Having and living that "good and contented life" will almost certainly create the environment for you to be happier, live longer and to remain in good health.

As mentioned before, money is not ultimately going to make us happy. If you decide to leave your current job, perhaps train or retrain to do something that really interests you and are passionate about, then chances are, you are going to be considerably happier than remaining in a tedious job just for the money, being stressed out and complaining all the time.

Consider the relationship between work, money and time to be free. Tally up the actual amount of money that you are earning, and then compare this with the actual money that you need to live comfortably.

Time is limited; our time on this planet is limited too; have fun, smile, find your passion ... and enjoy the journey.

- IF YOU HAVE ENJOYED THIS BOOK PLEASE GO TO THE AMAZON PAGE AND WRITE A SHORT REVIEW - https://amzn.to/2Jclatg - Thanks xxx

Further reading

Crushing It!: How Great Entrepreneurs Build Their Business and Influence-and How You Can, Too - Gary Vaynerchuk

The Inside-Out Revolution: The Only Thing You Need to Know to Change Your Life Forever - Michael Neill

The Road Less Traveled and Beyond: Spiritual Growth in an Age of Anxiety - Dr. M. Scott Peck

Blink: The Power of Thinking Without Thinking - Malcolm Gladwell

Richest Man In Babylon - George S Clason

Suggested films, talks and series

Groundhog Day

Love Actually

It's a Wonderful Life

Up in the air (2009)

The Fall and Rise of Reginald Perrin.

Documentaries on Netflix
    Dirty Money
    Sustainable
    Rotten
    Prescription Thugs
    Food Choices
    Fat, Sick and nearly Dead
    Take Your Pills
    Taste the waste
Documentaries on Amazon Prime
    Real Value
    The big Lie
    The flaw

Zeitgeist
End of the road
Food as medicine
Food matters
Super Size Me
Food inc.
Beyond Food

Suggested Ted Talks

Why I am done trying to be 'man enough' - Justin Baldoni

Why aren't we awesomer? - Michael Neill

Do schools kill creativity? - Sir Ken Robinson

The power of vulnerability - Brené Brown

All it takes is 10 mindful minutes | Andy Puddicombe

How to speak so that people want to listen - Julian Treasure

The puzzle of motivation - Dan Pink

About the author

Coach Antony Birks is a transformative executive coach and Business English trainer and teacher. He has, over the past 30 years, been mentoring and coaching a diverse international audience … and from all structural levels - from those who work on the shop-floor, to middle managers, top executives and CEOs.

Coming from a working-class area of London, and at the age of 30, he left England with his Bachelor of Science and moved to Germany – a place that he enjoyed as a child and now the place he calls home. His goal and role as a coach and teacher - after having experienced losing everything that was dear to him - is to now bring "the best out" of the people who he works with – with this being a passion; meaning that, most of the time, it certainly does not feel like "work" in the usual sense to him.

Coach Antony is best known for his new book:
"SMALL TALK – Enlightening Interruptions",
which is widely regarded as offering suggested thoughts about life to those with little or no time in our apparent hectic and fast-moving society.

As described in his latest book – SMALL TALK - is full of a multitude of difficulties and challenges, and, as so, Coach Antony is now, once again rising from the ashes. This rise, fall and rise have made him re-examine once again his passion with a new light. Being in the third stage, from within Joseph Campbell's Hero's Journey, this puts him in the last section – The Return ... where he now wishes to share his "treasure" with this international audience; enlightened readers; and others ... who are just willing to listen and perhaps learn.

He now lives, writes and teaches in Hannover, Germany. His sense of purpose – his *raison d'être* – is now mainly concentrated on his aptitude to teach; his further curiosity to study sociological, psychological and philosophical change; and his general passion for writing. His lifelong experiences have highlighted for him what is now essential and what is no longer important. Therefore, creativity has always been necessary for him ... be it painting, writing or photography. He offers his 6-week online course – which is solely based on his latest book – for people and organisations that wish to consider an alternative to the status quo.

His profound yet taken-for-granted teachings and suggestions have assisted an international audience to gently find solutions ... where they were hidden or masked beforehand.

Antony is a kindly spoken but prolific public speaker and writer, addressing organisations and companies using his directness and giving his alternative keynote speeches.

Coach Antony's website: www.coachantony.com Please click on the "event button" for Antony's courses and future public engagements.

Website:
http://www.ReachingHolisticChange.com
and
http://www.coachantony.com
Facebook:
 http://www.facebook.com/reachingholisticchange/

Twitter:
http://twitter.com/coachantony/

If you have enjoyed this book ... please leave me a review ...
here https://amzn.to/2sojraX

Recipes

The following 7 dishes (one for each day of the week) are presented below to offer you something easy, quick and nutritious to prepare and eat at home. If you are not used to preparing your own food, eating salads or fresh produce, you might find it advantageous to swap or exchange just **one** of the recipes below with your regular meals. Our bodies (and minds) normally need a little time to adjust to something new ... so be prepared to experience stomach aches, diarrhoea, etc. at the start. However, over time, your body will adapt to eating good healthy and nutritious food once again, and you will feel an overall general improvement in the shortest of times.

The proportions and recipes are generally for two people – and it assumes that you are not familiar with cooking. For this reason, make sure that the kitchen is neat, tidy and clean beforehand; this is really important – if you have not been using the kitchen recently and so that the food you prepare is hygienically ready to be prepared, cooked and/or served. Always make sure that you have the right ingredients at home, together with the correct amount of fresh vegetables and fruit. Do not forget that taking that extra precaution and washing the products (when you get them home) is always a smart idea. If possible, always buy locally produced produce and, if you can budget it in, buying organic and free-range food is even better (for taste and animal welfare reasons).

-

BREAKFAST:

The easiest and best breakfast is **oatmeal** (rolled oats) or porridge in the morning. Add one cup of rolled oats, oatmeal or porridge flakes to a pan. Add one cup of **water** and one cup of **milk**. Heat for three minutes – stirring the whole time. Mix in some grated fresh ginger (optional).

Dice an apple, (or plum, or pear, or any other piece of fruit) – add some honey (from a local bee-keeper), a few dates or figs to sweeten if necessary. Cover the fruit with the porridge – eat while hot.

Early morning quick and tasty porridge with fruit.

THE BASIC MIXED SALAD:

Portion for two adults. Take the following washed ingredients and cut them into large slices or segments:

- · 2 Tomatoes
- · ½ a Lettuce
- · 1 Celery stalk
- · a few Radishes
- · ¼ Cucumber

and put them into a large salad bowl.

Add sunflower seeds, sesame seeds, a few walnuts, a few red kidney beans (from a tin) and some cress to the salad or anything else you might have laying around the kitchen or fridge (such as dried cranberries, a tangerine, herbs such as mint, basil, parsley, etc.)

For all the salads mentioned below, occasionally try out new ingredients in your salads, to keep this new and exciting - and to find out which you most enjoy and which you do not. The following are alternatives:

Red/green/yellow bell peppers, avocados, parsley, carrots, beetroot, courgettes, mushrooms, grapes, Feta cheese, bean-sprouts, olives, kohlrabi, etc. There are also several types of lettuce. Different coloured vegetables, such as carrots, tomatoes, etc. which one can use to vary the appearance and taste of the salad.

-

THE SALAD DRESSING:

To make an easy salad dressing … just add two tablespoonfuls of extra virgin olive oil, one tablespoon of vinegar, a little salt and pepper to taste, plus a little mustard (optional). Mix these ingredients in a cup – add a splash of orange juice or a few drops of lemon or water, if too dry.

-

1. CHICKEN AND MIXED SALAD

Firstly, take an oven-proof ceramic bowl or dish. Add a tablespoonful of olive oil. Now wash the two chicken legs under the tap or faucet. Pat dry and lay them in the cold bowl or dish with the oil. Season with salt and pepper and add a clove of garlic. Turn the chicken over and add more salt and pepper – making sure that both sides are coated with the olive oil and the seasoning.

Cook in a medium/hot oven at about 170° C. (340°F. Gas Mark 3) for about 70-90 minutes – turning every 25 minutes or so. Cook until brown and cooked through – the meat should *almost* leave the bone.

While the chicken is cooking prepare *Basic Mixed Salad* (see above).

Mixed salad with organic chicken

When the chicken is fully cooked, add the *salad dressing* to the salad and gently mix ... then serve onto a plate. Place one of the cooked chicken legs on top of the salad ... and serve. If you are on a calorie-controlled diet, you might like to remove the chicken skins before serving and also consider those ingredients

156

which have a high-fat content.

2. LAMB AND MIXED SALAD

Firstly, take a glass bowl or kitchen dish. Add a tablespoonful of olive oil. Now wash the pieces of lamb (chops or loins are the best), pat dry and place in a bowl – marinate with a little olive oil, mince sauce, salt and pepper. Place on an oven grill and grill under a medium heat in the middle of an oven for approximately five minutes. Make sure that there is a tray under the grating to catch the cooking oils.

Prepare the *Basic Mixed Salad*. When the lamb is fully cooked (please do not overcook lamb), add the *Salad Dressing* to the salad and gently mix ... then serve onto a plate. Place one or two of the grilled lamb cuts on top of the salad ... and serve with mint sauce.

Mixed Salad with Lamb

3. SEAFOOD MIX AND MIXED SALAD

In a large frying pan heat a little butter and olive oil. Add a diced onion and a pressed clove of garlic until lightly brown and tender. Add 200 g of Fruit de Mare or shrimps and/or calamares and cook until the shrimps (3-4 minutes) have turned pink. Season with a sprinkling of dill, pepper and a little salt.

Prepare the *Basic Mixed Salad,* perhaps using Rucola/Rocket or Lamb's lettuce instead of the usual lettuce. When the seafood is fully cooked (please do not overcook the shrimps), add the

Salad Dressing to the salad and gently mix … then just before serving, add the warm seafood to the salad and serve onto a plate.

Mixed Salad and Seafood

4. TUNA & EGG AND MIXED SALAD

Prepare the *Basic Mixed Salad* Serve on a plate and add a warm boiled organic egg (cut in half and seasoned with a little salt and black pepper).

Get some good quality canned or tinned tuna, in water is the best and having only about 100 calories per serving – this is also good for your weekly dose of iron and potassium. Consider, too, if the brand or company considers issues such as source, heavy metals and sustainability, such as: Wild Planet and Sustainable Seas.

Mixed Salad with Tuna and Eggs

5. EASY SPAGHETTI AND SEAFOOD DELIGHT

Heat a large pan of boiling water, add a teaspoon of salt and a splash of olive oil to the water. Place approximately 200-250 g of spaghetti into the water, making sure that after a minute the spaghetti is fully covered (without breaking them) and then cook for approximately 10 minutes (or see packaging) or until firm to bite (*al dente*).

In the meantime, heat a large frying pan with a little butter and olive oil. Add a diced onion and a pressed clove of garlic until lightly brown and tender. Add a few halved cherry tomatoes together with a few sliced mushrooms. Add 200 g of Fruit de Mare or shrimps and/or calamares and cook until the shrimps (2-3 minutes) have turned pink. Add a handful of baby spinach and continue cooking for another 2 minutes. Season with a sprinkling of dill, pepper and a little salt.

Prepare the *Basic Mixed Salad,* perhaps using Lamb's lettuce instead of normal lettuce. Add the *Salad Dressing* to the salad and gently mix.

Then drain after the cooking period and add the seafood mix to the pan. Stir gently ... add the seafood and spaghetti to the salad and serve onto a warm plate.

Mixed Salad with Spaghetti and Seafood

6. QUICK AND TASTY FISHERMAN'S PIE

Preheat oven to 200°C/400°F/Gas Mark 6. Wash, peel and quarter the potatoes and cook them in a pan of salted boiling water for about 25-30 minutes or until cooked (test with a fork). Add to a frying pan some diced onions, garlic and lightly fry in some olive oil for about 5 minutes. Cut the fish (Fruit de Mare is also optional) into chunks and add to the pan and season with a little salt, pepper and dill. After some 5 minutes ... add the zest and juice of half a lemon (no pips) together with some finely chopped chilli. Add a few handfuls of fresh spinach and allow to wilt for a minute. Remove from heat.

Drain the boiled potatoes, add 50-75 g of butter, some milk – salt and pepper to taste and then mash until light and creamy. Move the fish and the rest of the frying pan to an oven-proof ceramic dish. Cover the fish with the mashed potatoes and spread evenly with the back of a fork. Add some coarsely grated or diced cheese on the top. Pop in the oven and cook for about 30-40 minutes (until brown)- making sure that there is a baking tray under your oven dish.

Serves for 4-6 people ...

- 1000 g of starchy potatoes
- 100 g Cheddar cheese
- ½ a lemon
- ½ a red chilli
- 600 - 700 g a mixture of salmon fillets, haddock, perch or any other white fish from sustainable or organic source
- A handful (100 g) of shrimps or/and Fruit de Mare.
- olive oil
- a little butter
- a splash of milk
- 2 handfuls (250 g frozen) of fresh spinach

Fisherman's Pie with Spinach

Bolognese Sauce:

In a frying pan at olive oil, 1 small onion, diced 30 g of high-welfare or organic bacon (lardon) and thinly sliced garlic and slowly fry (about 10 minutes) or until soft and light brown. Add the 250g of mincemeat beef and 250 g of pork mincemeat (organic if possible) and fry until brown. Add a tin of tomatoes 400 ml, 400ml of good stock (such as Gefro), a little tomato purée and simmer for 10 minutes. Add fresh baby spinach until they disintegrate. Remove from heat.

7. QUICK AND TASTY WINTER LASAGNE

Recipe for six. Preheat oven to 180°C/350°F/gas 4.

Prepare the Bolognese sauce and remove from heat.

In another hot frying pan add 20g of butter, a little olive oil, diced onions and garlic, diced high-welfare or organic bacon (lardon) and heat for a minute or two, then add 2 tablespoonfuls of wholemeal flour and stir briskly with a wooden spoon. When it looks like a paste, slowly add the milk (800 ml) and stir vigorously for about 1 minute or until smooth. Add 50 g grated cheese and stir in. Add a little Worcestershire sauce, a little nutmeg and season with salt and pepper. Remove from heat.

In a large oven-proof dish, we want to layer the three cooked ingredients – beginning with the **meat**, then the dry lasagne sheets and then the special cheese topping. Continue until the dish is full (3 layers are ideal). End with the last covering of lasagne sheets and the cover with the sauce (if you do not seem to have enough mix the remain white sauce with milk) and add some more grated cheese (50 g) on top.

Bake in a hot oven for about 25-30 minutes or until brown and bubbling. (make sure there is a tray under the dish!)

The Bolognese sauce can also be used to make a quick spaghetti Bolognese. Remember that when eating something hot or warm - try to add something fresh, such as an avocado (halved, with lemon juice and salt and pepper) or the following ...

A QUICK AND EASY TOMATO, MOZZARELLA AND BASIL SIDE SALAD.

This recipe is for one person. Slice a large organic tomato into slices – removing the top and ends. Slice the mozzarella in the same number of slices. Wash and coarsely cut the basil leaves removing the thick stalks if necessary. Layer the tomato, mozzarella and basil and continue until complete (see photo). When completed drizzle a little olive oil over the dish and season with salt and pepper.

DESSERT:

Mixed Fruit Salad and Natural Yoghurt:

Wash and clean several of fruit – apples, pears, berries, bananas, oranges, pineapples, melons, etc. - into small bite-size pieces. Add a splash of orange juice and a little lemon or lime juice. Mix and serve with some 1% natural yoghurt.

-

Fruit Crumble:

Preheat the oven to 190°C/375°F/ or gas mark 5.

Wash 2 or 3 organic apples – quarter and de-core (leaving the peel on); Do the same with a pear, plum, etc. or whatever you have available in your kitchen. You can also get a bag of frozen mixed berries, which is very convenient. Put these cleaned pieces of fruit in a large saucepan, add one tablespoon of your favourite jam or marmalade, a few thin slices of finely chopped ginger, (perhaps some sultanas or currents) and 100 ml of natural fruit juice (or red wine) and cook for 10 minutes.

In a mixing bowl add 200 g of wholemeal flour, 100 grams of rolled oats (porridge flakes) and 50 g of brown sugar and mix. Add small pieces of butter (100 g) and rub this through your fingers until it resembles fine breadcrumbs.

Place the cooked fruit into a glass ceramic oven dish and cover with the rolled oats mixture. Sprinkle a little brown sugar on the top and pop into the oven for approximately 30 minutes (making sure that there is a tray underneath to catch any leakage).

Enjoy your food ...

If you enjoyed this book - I would appreciate it if you could rate it on the Amazon page - https://amzn.to/2Jclatg